Last Moon Dancing

Last
Moon
Dancing

Monique Maria Schmidt

A Memoir of Love and Real Life in Africa

Clover Park Press • Santa Monica • California • 2005

Clover Park Press • PO Box 5067 • Santa Monica, CA • 90409-5067
Visit us at: http://www.cloverparkpress.com

This is a work of memoir. Names have been changed to protect the privacy of individuals. All trademarks referenced are the property of their respective owners. Any reference to brand names merely reflects their presence during the story told here and does not imply any endorsement of products or sponsorship by them.

Earlier versions of some of the sections have appeared in *Coal City Review 2000*, *Prairie Winds 2004*, and the author's MFA thesis at Syracuse University, 2003.

SHUT DE DO, by Randy Stonehill, © Stonehillian Music (Admin. by Word Music, LLC), Word Music, LLC, All Rights Reserved. Used by Permission.

Library of Congress Control Number: 2004113743
Schmidt, Monique Maria.
Last moon dancing: a memoir of love and real
life in Africa / Monique Maria Schmidt.
p. cm.
ISBN: 0-9628632-3-8   13 digit: 978-0-9628632-3-3
1. Autobiography–Coming of Age–Peace Corps Volunteer–Mennonite–Teacher.
2. Peace Corps–West Africa–Benin–Teaching. 3. Teaching Abroad–Peace Corps–West Africa. 4. Women–American Women–Living in West Africa–1998-2000–Teaching Abroad–Western America Farm Life. 5. Travel–West Africa–Benin. 6. South Dakota–Farm Life–Mennonites. I. Title.
2005

First Edition 2005

Jacket design by Sun Son.
Map art by Barbara Doutrich Weeks.
Art consultation by Laura Kidd Kennedy.
Author photo by Mary Schmidt.

Published in Santa Monica, California.
Manufactured in the United States of America on acid-free paper.

For my mother who got me started
and for Beaker who kept me going.

In honor of Becky

"To be literate is not to be free, it is to be present and active in the struggle for reclaiming one's voice, history, and future."
–Henry Giroux

"Reading the world always precedes reading the word, and reading the word implies continually reading the world..."
–Paulo Freire

Contents

Maps

    Glazoué   viii

    Benin/Africa   x

Prologue   1

Parts

1	Twenty-Four Moons Rising	3
2	Twenty Moons Dancing	31
3	Eighteen Harvest Moons	81
4	Fifteen Moons Full	95
5	Ten Moons on Fire	115
6	Nine Moon Shadows	141
7	Seven Moon Beams	181
8	Three Moons New	205
9	Last Moon Dancing	215

Acknowledgements   222

Notes   224

Glossary   225

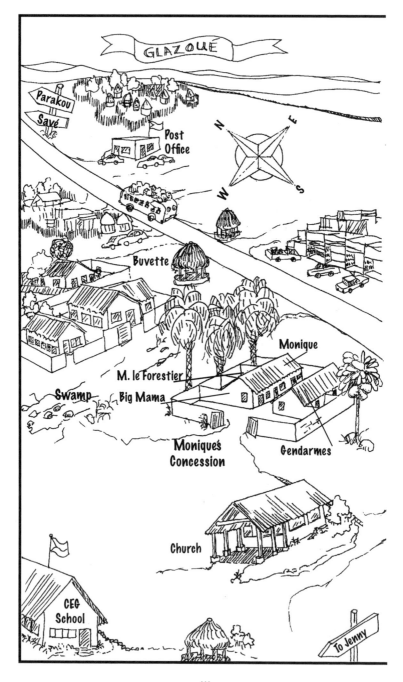

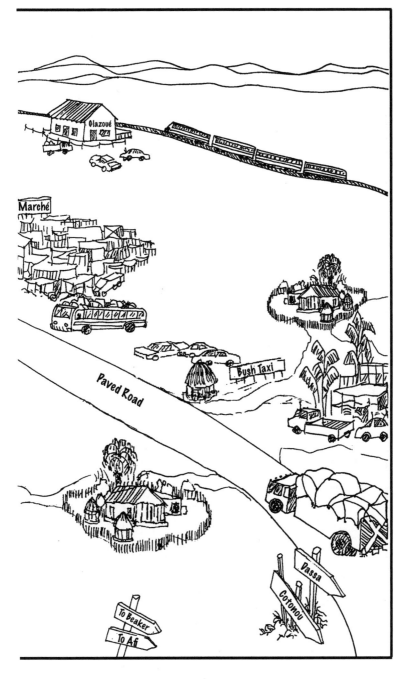

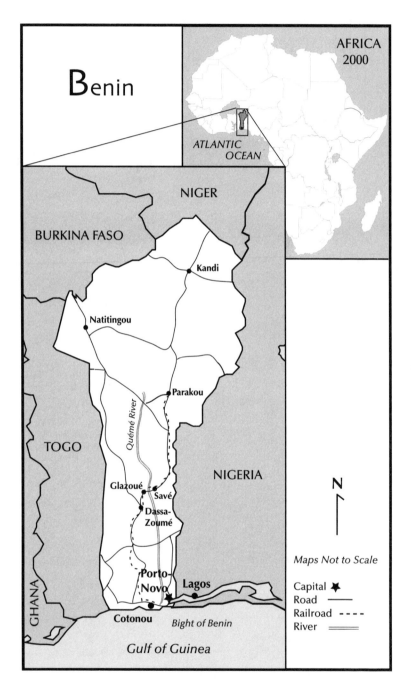

AFRICA
2000

Benin

ATLANTIC
OCEAN

NIGER

BURKINA FASO

Kandi

Natitingou

Parakou

Quémé River

TOGO

NIGERIA

Glazoué

Savé

Dassa-
Zoumé

N

Maps Not to Scale

Capital ★
Road ——
Railroad ----
River ═══

Porto-
Novo

Lagos

GHANA

Cotonou

Bight of Benin

Gulf of Guinea

Prologue

RR 2, BOX 105
MARION, SOUTH DAKOTA

THIS IS WHAT CAN HAPPEN. THEY CAN GET LOST. THE STORIES can get lost. You can shove them behind the mental grocery lists, behind the debate about whether to wear the *sugar 'n spice* lipstick or the *whisper #3* gloss. You can slip them behind the tears, smush them under the insecurity and then forget them. They will simmer. No, not simmer. They will tussle with each other, different versions taking different shapes and then trying to get out. Trying to squeeze themselves out of where you have shelved them with the reassurance that you will come back. Someday. Someday you will come back to them.

And then? Something will graze your skin, slide across your chest and find an open pore and slither into your veins, seeking your backbone, trying to twine itself around your vertebrae. A twinge. An echo. A sharp inhale. Fear. Silence will nourish it. The fear that you do not understand life. The fear that you do. The fear that there is too much unknown so you should not have a voice. The fear that you are unknown and have no voice. That you are foreign, even at home. That, for you, there is no home.

I usually joke about my years spent in a West African village, as if they were simply a sweaty, stinky, rat eating, tummy cramping adventure, as if Afi and the villagers hadn't given their homes, their laughter, their grooves, their children, their food, their lives, as if they hadn't given and given and given their strength, their love, their spirit—concocted with a little mango breeze, some *marché* dirt, and a little Nigerian palm oil—bounded and danced and *lived*.

So did I. With wind wrapped around my stomach, the sun scorched freckles on my skin. I danced at night under raving stars, living in the wild with God.

1

Twenty-Four Moons Rising

Boîte POSTÀLE 91
GLAZOUÉ, BENIN

Dear Angela,
    The medical unit trained me to look at my poop:
    -brown and solid = good
    -brown, somewhat solid with white specks=worms
    -yellow and mushy = not really a problem
unless you have a fever
    -mushy and fluorescent green = too much grape
Kool-Aid from care packages
    -fairly liquid and yellow, with fever = drink
lots of water
    If it feels like you're peeing out your ass,
don't use the glossy ads in the magazines to
wipe because they only spread it around.

Home is foreign. Here, nights smell.

Wind waddles through the wooden slats of my window, accentuating the proximity of latrine maggots.

Big Mama's advice for intestinal problems: two whole cloves of garlic, every day.

Breathing, the mosquito net flutters around my bed, brushing the stuffed bat and voodoo beads. The moon rises to light the sand paths for the Oro dancers. A scent is held in the air. My body hurls itself onto the bed, the fetal position. Something oozes. From my interior. Not the garlic or the giardiasis burps. Fear.

Listen to darkness. It arrives as comfort
or evil.

How long until I mildew?

Breathe deep, breathe deep, hold for four, release. Breathe deep, hold, release. Breathe.

Sunrise. I leave my house for the chanting and bargaining—once other people's stories.

> FOR CHARLES
> *In a whirling twirling land*
> *of red voodoo gods,*
> *running and screaming crowds,*
> *confusion and chaos,*
> *I miss you*
>
> *I miss you*

As the first foreigner to teach in the village, I was aware of the impact of first impressions. I wrote for my students, in French, my rules and expectations as well as the reasons for studying English. Then I practiced.

French rang from the latrine.

French rang from under my mosquito net.

French rang ever so softly as I biked. I inserted calculated pauses, broad gestures, stern looks. My students would see their teacher as knowledgeable, confident, and in-control.

Monday, October 4th, off I biked and everyone I passed said, "Madame, today is the beginning of school."

I replied, "Yep, sure is."

Completely in my performance mode, I arrived at school, pretending to be thirty years old, married and a seasoned teacher of English. And the day began...with no classes.

Undaunted, on Tuesday I again woke up early, practiced my welcoming speech, grabbed my bike and headed for school. Those I met said, "Madame, today classes will start."

"Maybe," I muttered.

Arriving at school, I found a chaotic mass of 800 khaki-clad students. The ones who had walked didn't have to deal with the squabbles arising over whose rusty bikes got to be piled against the mango trees and whose rusty bikes were relegated to the dirt. The professors roared in on their mopeds, more or less missing the students whose grade-bribes had probably paid for the motos.

Eventually, in lines according to grades, a small city of khaki, shaved heads, and braids surrounded the flagpole to sing the national anthem. After I indignantly corrected the director for introducing me as "Miss" instead of "Mrs.," I settled into watching 800 students sweep the sand, gulping a cloud of dust with their every swipe. Classes would start tomorrow...or the next day, depending upon a thorough cleaning of the school-yard.

The schoolyard: a large rectangle of sand, once covered with grass, which the community had burned off to keep away the snakes. My school: squares of concrete with tin roofs that popped with the heat of the sun and made classes impossible during heavy rains. The classrooms: no doors or lights, some blackboards and desks.

By noon, I was in a daze, having spent the morning trying to figure out whom to greet and whom to sit by and whom not to sit by, all depending on status. In training, I had learned that very important people associated only with other very important people. My problem? I hadn't quite figured out where I stood in those ranks. I was an American, therefore, somewhat important. But I was a woman living without a man, which almost cancelled out being an American. So I shook hands with some VIPS, like the director, and simply nodded to others.

Then there was the question of names. Most answered to titles, such as Mr. The Director or Mr. The Disciplinarian. I never knew if I could say, "Hi, Jacques" or if I had to say, "Hi, Mr. The Man Who Sells Nails." However, I took to this idea and did some naming of my own: Mr. The Man In Gray With Wide Haunches, Mrs. The Woman Who Thinks I'm A German Nun, Mr. The Man With The Indiana Jones Hat, and Mr. The Man Who Thinks His Line, "if you marry me, you could stay in Benin forever," will work.

In 100^0 noontime heat, I headed for the concrete slab designated for our teachers' meeting and the ominous promise of food. Neither thinking in French nor conjuring mounds of cooled fresh fruit could protect me from the effects of the spicy African offerings.

Other volunteers had forewarned me of my impending struggle as a woman. I needed to become a credible part of the school community, and this meeting was an important first step. *Monsieur le Censure* and *Monsieur le Surveillant* stopped me to point out I had *quelque chose* on the back of my dress. Puzzled, I twisted my head around and pulled the back of my dress towards the front. I froze. Red. At this moment I did not need to be reminded of my womanhood. I hadn't had a period in over two months because of stress and a lack of protein. I had forgotten about it. Now before my first teachers' meeting it had chosen to remind me of its existence, and it had done so with vengeance on the back of my yellow dress.

I said I must have cut my leg biking to school, and when I sat down, my dress must have brushed against my leg. They nodded solemnly. I said I should probably skip the meeting and go home to take care of the cut. They agreed.

Biking the distance back to my house in this condition was not going to help my predicament. At home I would have to dismount the bike and walk at least 100 feet in front of my neighbors before I could unlock my door. I had no choice. Accepting the lesson in humility, I biked back to my house, strode quickly to the door, greeted Big Mama and the kids tersely, went inside and cried.

Africa continuously reminded me I did not control my body. In the States, I rarely thought about my body and how it functioned. As a young, healthy person I had the privilege of ignoring it or making a novelty out of it. On the tedious trips from South Dakota to Kansas, my sister and I played bladder games to see who could go the longest without peeing. Out of sheer stubbornness I usually won. I continued my reign as bladder queen in college. At parties, I always broke the seal last, proudly becoming known for this skill. I flaunted it during the welcoming parties our first week in Africa, using the latrines less than anybody else.

However, it took Africa only a short period of time to smash my pride. After our first week of training, Peace Corps placed us in home-stays. My host dad was a local doctor, but even his family didn't have indoor plumbing. Their latrine stood about fifty feet from the house. At night, using it required untucking the mosquito net, lighting a candle, unlocking their door, and proceeding at a snail's pace in order to protect the flame. A normal latrine trip could take more than twenty minutes, after which I was too awake to go back to sleep. After my first night venture, I decided I would hold 'til morning.

Soon after I made this decision, I was tested. Several mornings later I was awakened by my host mother's making of the breakfast fire…and my gurgling bowels. My bladder twisted and flexed in revolt. It screamed for release. I sat up, viciously scrunching my muscles as I ripped the mosquito net from around the bed.

I swung one leg over the edge and stopped. With great deliberation I swung the other leg onto the floor, rose to my feet and hunched, momentarily frozen. From the floor, I grabbed the plastic baggy that had held my care-package Oreos and fumbled with the zip-lock. I opened it wide, spread my legs and simultaneously shoved the bag up. The anticipation released Victoria Falls. In seconds the zip-lock filled with the heavy odor of ammonia and brownish urine before splattering on the floor. My host mama heard my liquid gush into the plastic and knocked on the door. "Monique, are you all right?"

"I'm fine." I said as I gingerly zipped the bag closed and wrapped it in a towel. That night I would take it to the bucket shower area and throw it, and part of my dignity, down the latrine.

People wrote to me asking why I had come. After days like that one, I asked myself the same question. I knew that I wanted to be consumed by the intensity of living. But I had miscalculated the mental and physical effort required to become immersed into this environment.

Some of the volunteers, oblivious to poverty in America, chose to see it in an outside setting. They came to Africa to experience poverty, figuring that by living the complexity of simply being poor, with the added benefit of adventure and a definite date ending their foray into others' lives, they would gain some kind of wisdom.

By American standards the volunteers were poor. By the standards of the French government workers, the PCVs represented the untouchables of the Caucasian world. Most of the villagers saw the volunteers as characters in a strange drama, a drama of which they themselves were being asked to participate. Peace Corps caused ripples through their lives, and their lives rippled mine more than they could have imagined. No one in Glazoué knew how I could help anyone of them; yet they let me fumble around their doorsteps and rummage in their *marché* in my quest to become some kind of strong woman.

In college I sat in the sunlit cafeteria, hands encircling a hot cup of cocoa mulling over the concept of stripping my soul of everything that I used to define myself: material objects, friends, community, culture and language. By so doing I could learn. Studying in France had been my first attempt. It stretched me intellectually and improved my wardrobe, but I needed more.

So, I went to Africa.

And it humbled me.

Perhaps I was strong for living in the unknown.

Perhaps it was easier.

Dear Angela,
    French classes really help. Beaker's progress:
"I finished class, biked back to my host family and, using my new textbook French, I asked them how they were doing. They replied, 'macaroni.'"

REFILLING THE WATER JUG
Afi—from stone to stone
first right foot then
left foot searches

the rock for the
indentations

that will allow
one leg to stand
firmly with all
the weight of a fourteen

year old with a
twenty liter
basin of water

not sloshing, not
even dripping—
barely steadied

by a calloused
palm on her head,
across the yard,

up the path, knee-
high in the dust,
to the wooden

door of Beaker's
house, stopping and
turning her neck,

eager to see
the water again
and the ground which

now plays with a new
white girl, arms splayed
like Jesus on

the cross, skirt hiked,
sandals muddy
already, words

in a strange tongue
crashing over
the frogs and weeds.

When I reach
Beaker's door,
gathering dust

between my toes,
wiping my sweat
with a blue rag

taken from a
bag carried on
my back, Afi

squats to empty
her basin, I
smile with a soft

"bonjour." Afi
nods in reply,
then laughs her way

back to the source
to get her second
basin of water.

One hundred and ten degrees plus the body heat index. For Beaker it was like wrapping up in a sheet of plastic and sitting in the backseat of a stalled car with closed windows at three p.m. in Arizona. Hours passed slowly in a bush taxi listening to a chicken's claw scrape repeatedly across her backpack. Too scrunched between a *marché* mama who heaved-flopped her breast on Beaker's shoulder and a bag of *garri* to turn around and smack the chicken. Too dehydrated to yell, "Please, get your chicken off my bag." Nonetheless, Beaker arrived in Glazoué for her first visit. I joyfully helped her scrape the chicken shit off her backpack.

Beaker, nickname from the Muppets, made up for what she lacked in height with energy. The day after we swore in as official Peace Corps Volunteers, we listened to our country director's pep talk about nobly accepting challenges, overcoming hardship, making a difference, and living life without reservations. All the volunteers zipped up their duffel bags, filled their Nalgene bottles, strapped on their Tevas, and flagged down bush taxi drivers to roar off into the African bush and save the world from poverty. Excitement. Anticipation. A head rush of immortality. Not for me. Or for Beaker. As the volunteers shoved chocolate bars into the side pockets of their bags and double-checked their supplies of Marlboros, Beaker and I slunk off to a corner room in the abbey, where Peace Corps had lodged us for the weekend, and locked the door.

Our three-month training had included proper latrine usage, hand scrubbing of clothes, green mamba anti-venom kit use (there was only one in-country...five hours from my proposed site...but I knew how to use it should I still be alive when I reached the capital), and videos of volunteers who had turned HIV positive while in-service because of unprotected sex with host country nationals. They were college educated Americans. They knew about the mortal risks. They said they were lonely. They said we had no idea what lonely was. They said the English language had no word for *lonely*.

In Minneapolis, I had talked with a Peace Corps recruiter. After stressing over my interview clothes for a week, I arrived in the office in khaki pants, hair in a low ponytail, and no eyeshadow. I expressed my desire to challenge and improve myself by immersing myself in a diverse community and helping the people.

My recruiter looked at my résumé, saw my employment as host of Fox Channel 17 Kids' Club and told me living conditions would be rough. I might get dirty. I told her I grew up doing farm work. And I had been camping. It wouldn't be a problem. I also mentioned Thoreau.

Courageous, motivated, altruistic smiles of American volunteers laughing with villagers. I had glanced through the many red, white, and blue pamphlets she gave me. I read the quotes of volunteers. It had been tough. There had been obstacles. There had been sacrifice, but lives had been changed, both theirs and the villagers. Ten minutes later, I left to get my fingerprints taken so I could clear the background check and sign up for two years of growing, giving, learning, teaching, and proving my "toughness."

On the east coast, Beaker had been doing research with rat vaginas. She had an obsession with infectious diseases. Her ivy-league education, Ernst and Young friends, and Cape Cod foundation could not distract her from the allure of Africa. Two days after we arrived in Benin, Beaker was the first trainee to get sick. After fainting during breakfast, she spent several days in the hospital fighting an intestinal infection. Her study of tropical infectious diseases was no longer limited to books.

Three months of living in-country had filled in a lot of subtext the recruitment materials lacked. It had also highlighted a lot of what we lacked. No way in hell were we shipping off to some Godforsaken mud hut with snakes and no electricity. Schisto filled ponds and no doctor. Chanting locals and no grocery stores. Dog sacrifices and no telephones. Goat head dinners and no toilets. Beaker and I agreed we needed at least one more night in the capital to make sure we were the tough girls we wrote about in our letters home.

At ten p.m., a janitor came to clean the room and left perplexed as to why he had not been told that the Peace Corps needed the corner room an extra night. But not too perplexed. Five hundred francs helped clear up the confusion.

The door stayed locked and we stayed inside, sweating and without food. Self-made hostage situation. Who knew when all the Peace Corps staff would clear out of the abbey. Better to disappoint the tummy than to have the director of Peace Corps lose faith in his troops on the day after swearing-in. After all, we had sworn in an oath that we had no mental reservations about our service.

Three months later as we brushed through darkness on our way back from my favorite *tchouk* stand, we decided that the oath was an example of the American government's sick sense of humor. Beaker's visit to Glazoué happened to occur during one of my neighbor's drinking binges. My neighbor had introduced himself as *Monsieur le Forestier* though I hadn't seen any forests around in which he could work, and he didn't seem to like nature. He did, however, like palm wine and tall, full figured women.

When he mixed his palm wine with the women, he created a ruckus that lasted days. He'd saunter through the red gate of our concession, past the yellow concrete of the *gendarmes'* house, leading some colorfully dressed mademoiselle. Quicker than an ice cube melting at three p.m., all eleven children who normally shouted and chased tire rims around in front of my door simultaneously melted into the back rooms of their houses.

It was a trade off. During his drinking binges, no children screamed *"Allez! Allez!"* I never heard the clatter of rusted metal on concrete. Instead *Monsieur le Forestier* yelled incessantly.

"Akala! Akala! Get me some more wine!"

Frequently, Akala, my student and neighbor, intently watched beetles breathe and would not notice me struggling to carry a basin of water on my head. When *Monsieur le Forestier* yelled, she became even more engrossed.

"Akala! Damn it! I've got company and I need wine! Akala! *Viens!*"

"Fulberte! I need more wine! Fulberte! *Viens! Viens!*"

Fulberte, Akala's younger neighbor, had a passion for beetle breathing as well.

"Goddamn kids! Pelagie! Pelagie! Goddamn you, Pelagie."

"Wine! Dona, I need wine! Dona, you little *impolie,* come here and get me wine!" His intake of palm wine made him sway in the doorway, but he still remembered the names of all eleven kids.

"Fofo! Fofo, get off your goddamn mat and get me some wine! *VIENS ICI FOFO!*"

By day two of his spree, it had dwindled to just names.

"Francis! Fraaanciss! *Viens,* Francis!"

"Goddamn it, Rachidi! Goddamn. Rachidi!"

Correcting papers in my house, I cursed the big first world corporations that had contributed to the deforestation that now gave *Monsieur le Forestier* so much free time. Eventually, the constant "Akala! Fofo! Dona! Goddamnkids! Francis! Rachidi! Fulberte! Roland! Armandine! WINE! Salifou! Ines! Pelagie! Damn you!" drove me to leave the concession in search of my own palm wine or *tchouk.*

After the chicken-shitting, shoulder-as-breast-holder bush taxi experience, Beaker did not want to listen to his yelling either. We grabbed our sweat rags and left my house in search of our own beverages.

Tchouk: good stuff, millet beer served in a gourd. Not necessarily tasty, but magical. A couple of swigs and biking through sand in a frumpy dress in 100° weather seemed like the coolest thing to do. Two more full gourds, courtesy of the Nigerian flip-flop salesman next to us on the log, and it was the kind of thing we wanted to do forever. Who wants cars? Not us! Who needs air-conditioning? Wimps! Did Beaker miss fresh lobster dipped in butter? No! Did I care that my constant sulfur-smelling farting due to giardiasis was a major dating dilemma? Absolutely not! Would I want to date someone that shallow? What does *Vogue* know about fashion? Nothing! Why would we ever want to shower, shave, and wash our hair? We were starting the trend that *au naturel* was the hottest scent! And phones? What good were phones? Did humans ever really, truly communicate with each other?

Ah, yes, *tchouk*, inspiration in liquid form. The catalyst for all great thought. It provided me with many magical, moonlit walks on the dirt path from the *tchouk* lady's stand back to my house.

On this particularly divine walk with Beaker, we made a scientific discovery: the power of frogs. Outlined in moonbeam, I saw a frog. The *tchouk* in me thought he'd be a good friend. With one deft move, especially impressive considering I was coming from the *tchouk* stand, froggie joined the rice and mangoes in my bag. Quietly, so as not to draw attention to the movement in my bag, Beaker and I snuck inside my house. Things had not changed.

"IMBECILE! Salifou, am I not your elder? Get me some wine!"

Ignoring the commotion next door, Froggie, Beaker, and I proceeded to prepare to star gaze by unrolling my straw mat in the part of my house that didn't have a roof that was attached to the part of *Monsieur le Forestier's* house that didn't have a roof. The same stars that shown down on us shown down on him and his mademoiselle. The same bat that flew over our heads two seconds later flew right over *Monsieur le Forestier's* head too. The same frog that left my hand with a gentle toss landed, thud, next to *Monsieur le Forestier.*

"MERDE! *C'est quoi?* Where did it come from?? Get me a stick. Quick, give me that stick."

We giggled as one of the classic battles ensued: man vs. nature.

Whack—whack

"Ribbit"

"*MERDE!*"

Whackwhack—whack

"Ribbit."

"*Mon Dieu!*"

"Ribbitribbitribbit"

WHACK!

"Ribbit"

Monsieur le Forestier clapped in front of my door the next morning. Agenda: frogs. I agreed that normally frogs do not appear suddenly in the middle of the night, especially from out of the sky. Flying frogs merited concern. *Le Forestier* felt someone had cursed him. The person had taken the shape of a frog in order to gain access to his house and do him harm. I agreed to take extra precaution in shutting the gate at night to prevent frogs, even flying frogs, from entering his house.

As Beaker packed up her bag and I waited with her by the road until she flagged down a bush taxi with only human passengers, we decided that while rat vaginas, infectious diseases, and personal growth appealed to us, so too did the continued study of the before unknown link between the human psyche and frogs.

*The night we moved to the farm I
was half asleep. My mother carried me
into the entry. It was painted
blue and the walls were covered with flies.*

She was such a good mother,
such a good woman that she cried
outside behind the silos. I looked
at the Sears catalogue
in my room. My sister read
Harlequin romances and dreamed
of I don't know what. I swore
that when I went to college I
would wear the shortest skirts
possible.

My mother mixed the milk for
the bottle lambs and sent me
to the barn to feed them. Then
she made dinner for my father.

Look, a ten-year-old—in his too-big, torn, rumpled khaki uniform, machete scars, infected bug bites, spider-web-thin legs, and calves, dusty from the walk, four miles, to school on dirt paths. No shoes, no pencils, no books.

Hard to know Ikilou from this photograph—no smile, hungry stare, unloved, the twelfth of seventeen from Papa's three wives, and Papa's pockets held no francs, so he struggled, but still gave to Ikilou—mostly beatings.

His brothers beat him, the *marché* goat vendor beat him, the school director beat him, until Ikilou's eyes became fat with tears which dropped off his bony cheeks.

My deprived, forsaken student, Ikilou. He cursed me in Fon. A waif, who walked in my class wielding a machete. A less-fortunate one, who scraped charcoal damnations on my front door, sold me rotten mangoes for the wrong price, mixed oil and powdered bones to make *gris gris* that would give the next three generations in my lineage nasal warts and goiter.

Ah, yes, dear little Ikilou.

What happens if
you take the sea away
from the fisherman?
On the prairie, the sea exists
in the waving wheat
fields, rippling trees
on homesteads.
My dad made himself
a city man married
to a city woman.
Inside him, corn roots shriveled
then spread themselves wide
and ripped his heart.
He moved back to the open sky.
In a village of cotton fields,
sweet pineapples, corroded taxis,
and congested markets, what surges the souls?

At the marché
Mama Inez's red, yellow, and green foulard
cavorted around fifty-two charcoal braids
that danced behind her ears.
Inez hung off her skirt
only smiling with her eyes
until Mama Inez found fifteen francs.

Inez scrunched under the table
and out the door, looking for Mama Ikilou
slowly sauntering across sand paths
showcasing oranges balanced
in a lid of leaves on her head
which possessed neither foulard nor dancing braids

but a silent crew cut—
wild, winding, knotty,
dark,
an opaque darkness
where Papa Ikilou's fists
and curses found holes in the knotty paths
and seeped through to her eyes,
flaring her nostrils,
silencing her smile,
reminding Inez of the stillness
of her mama's braids
when papa came home.

Dear Angela,

In case you ever need to know: Monique's guide to successful sneaking of Kool-Aid and Oreos:

1. Remember to get the Oreos out from between your teeth before talking to the villagers; otherwise, they will think you have a disease. You can pass Kool-Aid off as medicine, but the Oreo medication story does not work.

2. Don't eat the Oreos right before eating traditional African food. What will happen is

you happily munch on Oreos—chocolaty, creamy—and then you sit down to an oily fish sauce and you have to engage WILL POWER to eat it. Then your hosts will ask you why you don't like their food, and what can you say?

3. Red Kool-Aid will be believed as medicine. Green Kool-Aid, no.

P.S. An interesting phenomenon: boogers. Dust and wind cause major nasal blockages. Not much toilet paper. A debate: can I afford to use several squares to relieve nasal congestion?

I was a changeling,
a river nymph,
sister to cheetahs,

singing fifty verses
of a homemade mantra,
insane with loneliness,
straight backed on a bench
against a concrete wall.

Tonight, not satisfied with star caresses
and moonbeam love. If the excitement
of a kiss would alight upon me,
would it shimmy along my fingernails,
groove into the lines of my hand, skitter
up my arm and over my collarbone
to settle in my soul?

Would the crickets hear me
smiling into the banana-tree breeze?
Would the mosquitoes see contentment
hovering and the cockroaches notice
my shoulders accepting a hug?

I, the African ballerina, the friend
of tadpoles, twin of dolphins, blew out
my candle and went to sleep
as I had for months,
without knowing.

HOW THE MENNONITE WOOED THE SORORITY PRESIDENT
(Monique's version)

GENESIS

South Dakota prairie—wind, dust, tractors, grease, lambs, and The Church.

EXODUS

She will have a name that is not found in The Books of Lineage. She will not know The Recipes nor The Hymns.

RUTH

Her mother-in-law shall wear lace-up shoes, in black, and long skirts and have forearms and biceps large from kneading bread.

ECCLESIASTES

She will not feel the excitement of The Family when The Church has The Christmas Social and her mother-in-law finds her a pioneer bonnet and makes *pfeffernüsse* and *zwiebach*.

JUDGES

Chapter IV, verse 18

Before The Social, The People shall stare when her children, half-bred, take communion while the other children, whose parents have told them that they are too young to know the Spirit of God, wait until fourteen, the age when His Spirit alights upon all.

verse 32

There will be money to buy soybean seed, possibly enough for a down payment on a swather, but her clothes will be from The Church's discard shop. When she does shop from the Sears catalogue, The People shall notice her new red dress as she places two dollars in the offering plate while her mother-in-law, in black lace-ups, places more in the hands of her father-in-law who lays it in the plate.

PROVERBS

God likes it that way.

ROMANS

Chapter VI, verse 8

The minister shall stand at the front of The Church with closed eyes, hands raised to Heaven, paunch from the *zwiebach* at last year's Social showing. He shall notice that her blond short-haired girls take communion again.

verse 9

He shall talk with her husband and her husband shall respond something about her backaches, her headaches, her frequent phone calls to a place called "Kansas" and people called "Methodists" who take communion from birth. Her husband shall suggest that maybe letting the girls take communion is a form of "salvation."

REVELATIONS

Her future husband shall tell her none of this, in that place called Kansas. He shall pick her up on his Harley, being, at that time, on a "leave of absence" from the Mennonites.

As she wraps her arms around his waist and presses close to him to avoid the burn of the wind, he tells her he likes it that way.

Dear Angela,
    I gave my students another fill-in-the blank
vocab test. Apparently a baker is someone who
repairs cars and a runway is the bride after the
wedding.

As I wheeled my boy's bike out of the house and grabbed the back hem of my dress with the front hem and prepared to lift my leg over the bar, the *gendarme* who had been sitting outside reminded me that I should wash my bike everyday. I agreed with him that I probably should. Almost all the villagers and my students told me the same thing, daily. However, my bike plowed through puddles and sand every day, several times a day, and I saw no point in washing it. I didn't have the extra time nor extra stamina for bike washing.

I woke up at six a.m., lit my lanterns and ignited the burner to boil water for tapioca. If I had cinnamon, I'd sprinkle it in the tapioca to trick myself into believing that brown specks in tapioca were cinnamon bits, not bugs. Then I graded a set of papers and biked off to school in my performance mode to greet the director and the other professors and my students. For four hours I wrote verb conjugations on the boards, made students stash their machetes, requested books to be opened, flipped through vocabulary flashcards, and anticipated noon and a three-hour break. Returning home, I'd change out of my frumpf-frumpf into just a *pagne,* dump water over my head from the water storage jug, swallow more tapioca, and slouch in a canvas sling chair, trying to conjure coolness seeping through my aquarium-blue walls. All too soon, I had to pedal back to school, teaching until seven p.m., even though darkness settled in at six, and for the final hour my students could no longer read the blackboard.

At the end of the school day, I biked to the little *marché* to check for miracles: bananas, pineapple or eggs. Usually, only onions and tomatoes greeted me, so back home for more tapioca and a wait for Akala or Pelagie to fetch me water for a shower. By then it was 9:30, and I still had to prepare for the next day's classes. No way was there energy to wash a bike, and besides, I didn't want to waste water on that activity.

This simple life I led wore me down. Before arriving in Benin, no one bothered to tell me that Thoreau took breaks from his noble experiment. And I don't think that he had to actually *look* for food and water. For me, just surviving was cause for fatigue. This simple life was not utopian, but rather the necessity of living in tandem with nature. There was no time nor energy for life to be anything other than focused on the basic necessities of living.

I smiled at Akala as she walked by in her khakis, heading off to school. My ever vigilant *gendarme* favored me with one of his famous proverbs (in all probability because I had not taken his bike washing advice): "Raising a girl is like watering your neighbor's plant." I looked at him, finding in his comment the necessary motivation to teach another day.

Motivation escaped me many days, and I wasn't particularly proud of myself. I had planned to defend women's rights and change the village. However, I hadn't had much practice being outspoken in America, and the idea of disrupting the flow of village life, without my usual support system, unnerved me. I conjured up scenarios of liberating speeches given on the steps of the school, male professors aghast as my voice crescendoed and I stormed out of the schoolyard in righteous indignation. But the idea of following through with that daunted me.

I drove myself to teach English, but the third unit in the PC issued textbook, which only a handful of the students had, spoke about movies. Had my students ever seen a movie? Where were they going to use the word *stuntman*? And the computer chapter followed the movie chapter. Sometimes the blank stares that faced me had nothing to do with understanding English, but they had everything to do with understanding the concepts. For them the context of these chapters was otherworldly. They could say, "A stuntman does dangerous things." But they couldn't say, "Kill the snake." Thus, a beneficial lesson directed at a student group familiar with things electrical became for my students a lesson in abstraction. No wonder their boredom led to discipline problems which tested my sanity.

When I first arrived, I had no idea how the system of discipline worked. Few listened in class. Most arrived late, slouched, passed notes, talked, waved machetes, or walked around–seventy agitated students amusing themselves by frustrating one *yovo* English teacher. One day the disciplinarian walked into my room and a kid sassed him. The resulting punch in the head and kick in the butt shocked me on a much different level than the shock I felt when a herd of goats meandered through, depositing droppings on their way out the other side of the classroom, right in the middle of my inspired vocabulary drill. I couldn't hit the kids, and they sensed that.

Even if it meant the lot of them, I decided to kick them out of class. This direct action made me a better teacher, or so I thought. Later I discovered that the students I had removed were further disciplined by being beaten or by being forced to cut grass two hours under the afternoon sun. I still kicked them out. I couldn't deal with the havoc they created if there were no consequences for their actions.

It only took me several weeks to get tired of the "but teacher I walked four miles this morning and my brother beat me and I haven't eaten." It was true about their walking miles to school and not having had anything to eat and getting beaten before, after and during. And during Ramadan they fell asleep in class because of fasting on top of their chronic hunger. But everyone walked four miles and got beaten and didn't eat. I was overwhelmed. So I just taught. And kicked them out.

The first week, I brought in stories on large pieces of paper. Two students would hold the paper in front of the class while I asked for volunteers to read. I pointed to a student and said, "Will you read?" Never did the designated student read. Instead a smallish boy in the fourth row popped up and read every single paragraph. After the third time, I said in French, "Please, let your classmates read." He nodded. I pointed to another student, "Will you read?" and the imp in the fourth row stood up again. The class laughed. I fumed, "Get out!" He looked at me incredulously, shaking his head. I repeated the order, "Get out!" and pointed to the door. He said if he left, he would get beaten. I told him he should have thought of that earlier. The class fell silent. He picked up his notebook and left.

He returned with *Monsieur le Censure* who wanted to know why I had kicked out a student for reading in class. Reading in class was not the problem, I replied. The problem was not allowing other students their turns at reading.

"The boy said that you called his name every time."

"Nonsense," I snorted. "I was pointing to other students and saying, 'Will you read?'"

The imp interrupted with "See. She said it. She said Wilfried."

Not long after this incident, the man in charge of discipline informed me that he would no longer be disciplining the students. A rash of curses spreading through the village frightened him, and he felt directly threatened. He wouldn't discipline them; I couldn't. That meant no more smacks aside the head or stints of cutting grass. Ideally, this was my objective as a PCV teacher. One goal reached. However, I couldn't take credit for the change, and now my classroom became a free-for-all. I cursed whoever had cursed the *Surveillant* and kicked out students who tried to be kicked out so they could gather behind the latrines and gossip about which girl had "studied" with which professor and why the *yovo* didn't wash her bike.

2

Twenty Moons Dancing

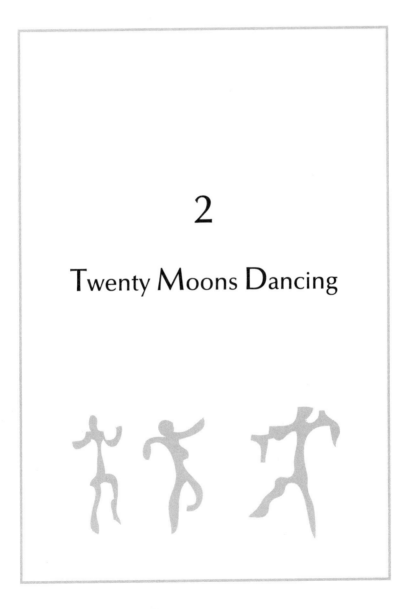

*G*OALS:
to be a dolphin, a water angel,
the luminance of heat lightning,

> *I felt along the concrete floor for the matches,*
> *knocked over my canteen. Noise reverberated,*
> *gelled with croaking frogs.*

a free floating cotton puff whipping around a smile,
the first rain drop to smack a dry palm leaf,

> *my pulse flew like the plane in my dreams.*
> *home in twenty months.*

the purr of a cat after a fish head snack,
the spirit of a savannah breeze,
the waft of butter sautéed garlic,

*twenty chances to dance naked
under the full moon. I memorized
my mother's letters, ventured into sleep
on the fringes of her memory.*

In school today, Ikilou's simile—the only correct one after two hours of class exercises—"Madame Monique is as fat as an elephant," pissed me off. Even though I wasn't fat by American standards, I was flabby in comparison to most of my students who had worked harder than I had growing up.

I biked home churning sand not only on the corners of the path, but as much as I could on the straight-aways. I only slowed down after I was inside the concession gate. Big Mama, Papa Rachidi's second wife, sat as she always did, with a basin of peanuts next to her. Naked, drooling kids—which I had almost run over—sat scratching pictures in the dirt just outside the gate. Not all the kids drooled. Only Francis, handicapped in some way, actually drooled. The other kids often had colds and therefore had runny noses, but Francis owned the title of "drool fiend." In my letters to America, I mused about the cause of his retardation, never mentioned his drooling. As a Peace Corps Volunteer, I felt I shouldn't notice his drool.

I swung open my door and shoved the bike inside to keep the kids from ringing the bell incessantly and strode over to Big Mama's mango tree to reiterate in angry French my newest reason to explain the underdeveloped state of Africa: insubordination. Big Mama listened, but she looked at the statement through a different cultural lens and considered the simile a compliment. Nonetheless, she tried to calm me by promising me a hearty portion of cow skin that evening.

During my third week in the village, Big Mama had told the *gendarmes* to quit peering through the windows of my house and pestering me about the absence of a husband. Since then I thought of her as a mother and definitely one of my few allies in the village; so I acted as if her cow skin remedy would work. I crossed the concession to my house, found my straw mat, went back to sit in the shadow of Big Mama as she switched from shelling peanuts to preparing cassava for Papa Rachidi.

MY FATHER'S PIANO
It was such a good piano
that it had an internal humidifier.
When the piano was dry,
a red light blinked on to say
it was in danger.

Red: danger, danger, danger, death,
death to the piano, death to the piano
and to Mozart and to Bach and to Bartok
and the Fifth Symphony and the Sixteenth.
The European continent was ruining
my childhood.

I used my French horn case
to block the red light. At night I left
the ceiling light on so the red glow
would go undetected. I tried to tip
the piano to one side and drain
the water out. Once, I gave it tea.

My mother did not compare me to Ghandi.
She bought a new metronome.
My sister promised to water the piano.

Peace Corps sponsored a three-day meeting between volunteer teachers and the Beninese teachers to discuss and resolve school problems. Rather lofty goals. Free cokes and real potatoes enticed most of the volunteers, and Beninese, to attend. The actual meeting, especially the session about educating girls, tested my self-control. When the session started, the native teachers, all male, swung into their long phrased fancy French about how they truly were trying to help girls get an education.

A volunteer from the north, where it was even harder for girls to go to school, asked the question I had been wanting to ask, "How does having sexual relations with the girls help them academically?" The denials, the non-responses, followed by the standard—"Girls can't learn. All women care about are their clothes and their hair. If a girl comes to school, she knows what to expect," reminded me of the many teachers' meetings I had sat through in Glazoué.

Like any kind of local gathering in West Africa, the faculty meetings in Glazoué were hot and long, and I had usually eaten carbohydrates before coming. I had opportunities to speak, but my speeches carried no weight. At first, sleeping through these meetings seemed the most logical activity.

However, after the first get-together, I never again entertained that temptation, not even to daydream. On that first time, the director laid out the rules for teacher/student relations, specifically sexual relations: 1) They could not take place at the *marché* because it was too "public" and their wives might see. 2) They could sleep with a girl who already had a boyfriend, but if there were problems, they were to be solved off school grounds. 3) They should try to sleep with only one student at a time.

No one used euphemisms to lay out the rules. No one worried that I might be surprised or offended. When I asked for clarification to see if they really meant *sexual* relations, they paused to laugh before continuing the meeting.

The faculty thought with the present rules, the school year would go smoothly. However, problems arose. *Monsieur Professeur du Histoire/Geo* rented a "study" room and invited girls there to "study." A math teacher thought this was inappropriate, mainly because he did not have a study room and, therefore, was losing out on opportunities to "tutor." The math teacher started chiding the geography teacher for his behavior. During his lecture he was interrupted by the geography teacher saying, "You, you, I know all where you and your testicles have been." Sentences such as this occurred frequently. They made me pull out my English/French dictionary to see if I had actually understood the sentence. Generally, I had.

The majority of my students had no dictionaries or textbooks where they could double-check information. The school did not, of course, have a copier; so I created most of the exercises for my classes by writing them on big pieces of brown paper for my students to read and complete in class. While using the names of my friends and relatives in the exercises to make me laugh and feel less homesick, I also tried to be subtly feminist.

On one of my exams I gave them a reading comprehension in which a woman, Angela, had a job in an office and became president of her company. In my reading comprehensions and class exercises, my women never swept or cooked or had babies. At the end of Angela's success story, I asked my students to write an essay giving their opinion of women working outside the home.

Ikilou wrote, "If your woman works outside the home, it is no good because you not know if she is sorceress. If you visit her with your motorcycle, you can have an accident. Women working outside the home is no intelligent."

His essay was enlightening. I had stressed that women were as *capable* as men, not realizing that the issue was one of sorcery, not ability. No wonder my conversations were so one-sided. I didn't even know the cultural assumptions.

I had the brainstorm of using myself as an example to prove that women working outside the home did not transform into sorceresses. However, I quickly reconsidered. In the present setting, the concept of sorcery contained power. Power I needed. By introducing a hint of sorcery into my persona, I had a secret weapon. Since several of my classroom exercises had been less than successful, a surprise, secret weapon could be a powerful ally.

```
Dear Angela,
     Things to ponder:
     1. the noise a tin roof makes as it expands
in the heat
     2. the number of people who can fit into a
five passenger car
```

I promised myself to write at least two good poems a week. However, as I struggled to capture Benin in my journal, the futility of encircling the workings of that world with my words made me snuff my candles, stretch out in bed and with my finger trace lines from mosquito bite to mosquito bite on my calf. Sleep escaping me, I untucked the mosquito net, struck a match for a candle and dug through my cache of letters, letters with careful reminders on their envelopes, letters read and reread, almost committed to memory. I sought out letters from my mom, her poems.

> THE BRAIDED RUG
> We transplanted your scruffy Kansas warmth
> to the battleship-green linoleum
> in the South Dakota farm kitchen.

38

Stretched in the shadow of the round oak table,
your garbled brown-toned lines lay witness
to eighteen years of meat and potato anchored meals.
    You stifled the fork's clatter,
    slowed the solitary pea,
    swallowed the milk's splash.

You cushioned ages of feet from nubby woolen booties
and puppy pads to Nike high tops and leather-cracked
chore boots. You caught bits of the seasons:
    purple eggshell fragments,
    one cherry pit, and
    gingerbread crumbs.

Good works count for nothing here.
Your fine grit tears touch me not.

I wrestle you to the trash pile and watch
the sad smoke spiral.

THE SHADE DREAMER
Three saplings keep a thin vigil
beside two field stones transplanted
in the circle drive between the house
and the barn. Atop each stone a small
girl waves to the straw-hatted
man seated on a sputtering WD 45.

With the loader-tractor he
rescues the rusted A-frame
from exile behind the machine
shed, resetting it among the young

trees. He dresses it in black paint
and completes the make-over
with bright chain and a
seven foot redwood swing.
Instantly claimed by two young girls,
it sways haltingly with their antics.
"Family-sized," he says,
standing in the growing shade.

One harvest follows another and
the man, straw-hatted still,
sinks to his place on the swing,
studies a preening cat in the
speckled shade, and
rests a calloused hand
on my knee…
     dreaming.

We had been living on the same farm in the same house, but I had no concept of her reality. She wasn't angry at being on the farm? She thought my father was a dreamer? Her poems seemed gentle and compassionate, starkly contrasting the every day routine of making early coffee for my dad and running through feedlots chasing errant sheep and fretting over payments to the bank. When did my parents feel this love for each other?

I never stopped wondering how exactly my mother had fallen for my father. I never thought about my parents being in love or really caring for each other. They were my parents, not real people. They said they loved each other, but the ways that TV portrayed love I never saw…no deep looks, no long kisses, no overnight trips to hotels while my sister and I stayed with a babysitter. But my mother had written poems about my father. Possibly she felt the same I felt for Charles?

It was bizarre to think of my mother wanting to hold hands and be smiled at in return like I did. It was strange for me to think of her searching out hugs from my father as I did with Charles. It was out of character to think of my mother as actually being in love. And my father? I didn't know where to begin. Had she giggled when he called?

And did Big Mama feel that way? Did being a second wife affect her? Was it really any different from the relationships some of my friends had? I often wanted to ask Big Mama questions about love and her situation, but never did.

I never quite felt like Big Mama's equal. Classwork, reading, videos, conversations, orientation—nothing taught the reality she lived. Among the village women, I was a strange child from a strange land.

Volunteers hanging out together dissected the nature of this love thing. The authors they quoted colored love in familiar shades. The rough, sometimes violent, life in the village seemed an unlikely place for love to flourish.

And then there was sex. I knew a lot about sex—sex for breeding animals. Unlike other farmers, Dad bred our sheep in winter for late spring lambing when he did not have to teach. I could strap a chalk-halter to the chest of a Montadale buck so that when he mounted a female, he left a clear, solid line on her back, thus proving his virility and her fertility. Our three bucks, each with his personal color-coded chalk, had to be rotated in and out of the 300 ewes so that they could rest and "restock." After months of isolation from the fairer sex, the first days' exposure to the ewes left the boys breathlessly scrambling over the frozen ground seeking access.

Now sex between humans was not so objectively handled. I always melted into the periphery when those conversations arose. During the health section of our orientation, the volunteers had to demonstrate to the nurse the correct procedure for condom use. That seminar took me back to Monsieur Perrin's

French translation class in which I had prayed, fervently, daily, "Please don't call on me. Please don't call on me." In Africa that prayer morphed to "Please don't make me put the condom on the dildo."

On trips in Africa, other volunteers and I often found ourselves sitting on our moto helmets beside the road, waiting for the bush taxi driver to find water for the radiator. I relaxed when the discussions drifted from physical details of coupling to the more intangible concept of love. In kindergarten, Mrs. Becker took away my recess privileges for kissing Dan on the playground and during nap time. In third grade Dan and I decided we were going to get married, until he told me I would have to wash his socks. I told him that I didn't wash socks. When Linda volunteered for the sock detail, my love compact with Dan ended. Love then and now perplexed me.

One book had described love as *the will to extend one's self for the purpose of nurturing one's own or another's spiritual growth.* That definition of love, maybe minus the word *spiritual*, seemed to fit in the village. Was this my mother's love? I imagined she would say no. Still, she clearly loved my father. He had been a world traveler, a scholar, a college professor, an intellect who raced his bike and read and discussed; but that was the father I didn't know. I, like, Spitz, our black lab, knew the man who farmed and taught full time and cussed on the weekends when the tractors broke.

I didn't know the man who on impulse paid a Parisian sidewalk artist to draw a caricature of himself smoking a pipe. For a long time, I saw that as just a picture hanging in his office. My dad didn't smoke, and he certainly wouldn't have spent money on a silly cartoon of himself.

I had a strange relationship with the people in my village. They respected my skin, didn't believe that I could teach them and saw me as a source of money. I resorted to lying in order to establish my credibility.

During a conversation under a mango tree in the waning days of my training, a veteran volunteer handed me a silver band, a symbol, she said, more powerful than any résumé or words of my wisdom. So, not as a single twenty-two year-old woman, but as a married thirty year old, I settled into Glazoué with my two bags of books and clothing, a mosquito net, mattress, propane bottle and a too large wedding band on my middle finger. In my first meeting with the director, I spoke proudly of my marriage to Spanish speaking Todd, of his dual pursuit of degrees in medicine and law, of planning a family when he finished with his studies, of his eagerly anticipated visit in December and, yes, the wearing of the wedding band on the middle finger, a sign of both our separation and our fidelity. His non-appearance in December was months away, plenty of time to revamp my story.

Luckily for me, Glazoué was situated about in the middle of the country, a convenient layover for volunteers on their way to and from the capital. During one two-week period, five volunteers stopped by my hut, four of them men. The number of visits flabbergasted my community. When the first young man showed up, the local men huddled together with smirks on their faces. After his departure, one of my neighboring *gendarmes* approached to politely ask if my husband had been visiting. I assured him that it was not December; the man had not been my husband, just a visiting American. By the end of the first week, my house had been a way station for two more male volunteers. To the village men I might as well have been spitting fire under the full moon. They fretted about the developing situation with sideways glances and tribal grunts. Ikilou told me they suspected me of running a *yovos* only brothel.

No woman, especially not a married woman, ever had more than one man. To Big Mama, I patiently explained the "just friends" concept, but in Benin a male and a female sleeping under one roof meant booty. My explanation evaporated before it reached her ears. She was wife number two to her husband.

That was OK. He was a man. For me, a woman, it was not good.

Two male volunteers wrote saying they wanted to use my house as a pit stop the following month on their way to the north. Two men at once. I would send my village into a coma.

WHEN WONDER WOMAN DIDN'T ARRIVE
Voiceless air dropped the drumming
from the marché outside Beaker's house.

Afi hugged me, then raised blistered hands
above her rumbling tummy to dance

between fallen branches—cascades
of heat lightning illuminated the sand

and blades of grass sardined between her toes.
She grinned. I laughed, waved to the moon,

let a cautious breeze revel in wrapping
around my clean skin.

Once, she told me a rotted rhythm
had pushed Papa Afi home.
Drunk on tchouk he stomped
blood out of her toes.

Afi had yelled.
Papa Afi had yelled.

I listened, sighed.

Come out ferocious soul, come
tell me where you go
when Papa Afi rampages
and no one, not the trees
nor the wind, dances.

Ikilou and Rachidi had been the first to ask me for names of correspondents. During my three-month training, current volunteers had explained never to give out home addresses or the addresses of friends. Students would skip lunches and work extra at the *marché* to save money for the overseas stamps and the envelopes in order to write letter after letter after letter until the mythical kind person in America sent them a plane ticket: writing could get them out of Africa, placing them in a land where they could have a green bike like mine.

Rachidi told me stories about the miracles of mail. In other villages, small gifts sometimes arrived. Even one magazine could nourish hope. If the American had spent money on a magazine full of pictures of houses and clothes and smiles and boys and girls hugging, surely, later, the envelope would contain the ticket for the plane and a new life. So, more lunches were skipped, extra bags of rice hauled at the *marché* and during the weekend, I corrected grammar in the letters to America.

Hectic American schedules consumed the time of my friends and family. When they took time to write letters, both they and I wanted them to be letters to me. But, the kids in my village wanted pen pals. The solution lay in World Wise Schools, a Peace Corps program that matched schools in third world countries with schools in the States. Since my mom taught geography, Peace Corps service became the ideal way to connect a small town in South Dakota with a small village in West Africa. Students in South Dakota could learn about Africa, and I could finally give my students an address for correspondence.

The escapade began. I didn't know if the American students liked writing to Africa or if my mom made them, but they wrote. Lots of letters arrived with drawings and pictures, but no gifts. I had told my mom to send nothing in the letters, and I had told my students they could not send letters asking for gifts. In my classroom, the letters provided a cultural exchange and a way to improve English, not a false fertilization of hope, or a cementing of the idea that material stuff made life better. Although, since I enjoyed the "stuff" people from the States sent me, I didn't instruct them to stop sending me care packages.

The situation perplexed the students in Glazoué. They laughed when they read the letters and enjoyed learning about hockey and baseball, but where was the money? The offers for adoption? The plane tickets? I explained the letters came from students, who had no money. "But what about their parents? Don't they have money?" Of course they had money, but not enough to send for another child. "But look at the pictures they sent me. They have whole blackboards in their school and they have big houses and one of them has a car. They must have money for me."

How to explain the way the world worked? People in America had different lives. People in Africa had different lives. The differences would remain. Sometimes I wanted to explain that the inequality they perceived was an illusion. America wasn't a better place to live simply because it was a "developed" nation. Life and people were not simply nicer because houses had carpeting. But how could I say that when I longed to go back?

And if I truly believed that their way of living was just as good as the American way, why was I helping them write letters to learn more about America? Why was I designing my English exercises around American values? Why did I ask my mom to have the girls write about playing sports and to mention that their brothers also did chores around the house? And when the kids in America received letters from me saying I missed America and that they were very lucky to live in our country, what were they taking from my words?

I argued about the intent and ramifications of Peace Corps with other volunteers, but we never reached a conclusion. And we were in Africa, in the midst of teaching, and we weren't going to quit; so those of us involved in the letter writing continued, silencing the inner debates and blindly hoping some good in some way was occurring to which we were merely oblivious.

The letters created another link in cross-cultural understanding. My students now understood why I hovered around the post office, why I hastily leaned my bike against the steps and bounded inside though ten minutes earlier I had barely been able to sum up the energy to thread myself over outstretched legs and muddy machetes to the back of the classroom to collect all the conditional essays on what they would do if they had 10,000 CFA. Mail: something from someplace else. Someone somewhere had thought about us.

With two broken chunks of chalk, I scraped the address for the seventh grade class in South Dakota on the blackboard at school, saying I would pay postage for the first letter each student wrote. Students asked about South Dakota's closeness to New York and about writing to Will Smith. (How they knew the Fresh Prince, I never knew.) Ikilou's stubby pencil fastidiously copied the address. He returned the next day before eight a.m. with a letter. I read it, suspected he had found a Nigerian from church to help him write it. While I liked to think I taught him solid English, I knew he had not mastered long prepositional phrases in my classroom.

Dear 7ᵗʰ grade class:

Being in a very great joy, this favorable chance is offered to me. By that I write you this small letter. In this, is included first of all my greeting to you and your whole family.

If you have my letter at this appropriate time, it is to inform

*you of things in Benin and about school and about how we are
enjoying life in Glazoué.*

*We started school at beginning of October. We have a very nice
school with many teachers. Our first school test is November 27ʰ.
Madame Monique said she has greeted you for me and that you
greeted me. Thank you.*

*This year I will pass my exam BEPC. So pray to God for me
to succeed at this exam. To finish, I wish you good and happy year.
May God bless you with his great blessing.*

*Your beloved friend,
Ikilou*

Class ended at noon. He waited for me at the school gate,
checking to see if I were heading to the post before buying rice
and beans to make sure his letter got placed in the dusty cloth
mailbag and then strapped on the back of the postmaster's blue
moto and then thrown on the train and then transported to
Cotonou and then to *America* so his new friends would start
planning for him and he could begin writing down instructions
for them on how to make *ignam pileé.*

Up and down the trunks of palm trees and over piles of
onions at the market, word spread. Other students heard that
Ikilou had actually written a letter, and I had actually put a
stamp on it and mailed it. They wrote letters too.

Neither Ikilou nor any of the other students had mailboxes.
However, the next day they started their daily noon vigil at the
post office. Chasing each other in their flip-flops around the
building, they waited for replies and checked to see what came
for me. I got packages, why didn't they? They wanted to check
to see if those packages that I picked up were actually for me;
perhaps I was taking their packages.

They swarmed also to survey when *Monsieur le Censure*
putt-putted up on his moped right before siesta to gather the
mail for the school. Beady eyes targeted and pierced the cloth

mailbag. Were there any letters in red, white, and blue airmail envelopes, distinctly different and infinitely more exciting than the mauve envelopes sold in Benin? And if so, after *Monsieur le Censure* picked them up from the post office, did they reappear at the school, or did they stay hidden in the side-bag of his moto to reappear later at an undisclosed location.

When Ikilou received a letter, he walked towards my classroom with more dignity than the bell boy. Letter groupies followed. However, Ikilou didn't want anyone to read his letter. He didn't open it at school. I knew he had the letter, but not until a week later did I see it.

At home, he had carefully sliced it open, but he hadn't understood it. He had kept it, waiting for me to teach him the vocabulary in class. Unfortunately, I didn't cover "cupcake" or "football cleats." Finally, he asked. The mystery solved. I thought he might have been disappointed to know the strange words described food and clothes, but he smiled and said he would write back about his school uniform and bean *beignets*.

LINGUISTIC COMPETENCE I

I. Write the correct preposition in the blank.

    1. _____ Tuesdays, he sits _____ a tree and talks __ everybody who is going ___ the market.

    2. During vacation, she wants to go _____Glazoué _____ America.

    3. His mother told him to come ____ Cotonou ____ train ____ Friday, the 18th.

    4. She put the book _____ her bag.

In South Dakota, my family went through a lot of dogs. Their short-lived tenures on our homestead became a tangible sign of the tenacity needed on the farm. How many dogs could die? Spitz, my dad's black lab, rode in the pick-up with us on the move from Kansas. Spitz knew the life where my dad had time to play with a dog, to take him swimming and throw sticks. He had had time and soul to wrestle and growl with Spitz.

Spitz died of old age while my dad taught and farmed full time. My parents buried him under the mulberry trees in back of our white farm house and put a stone from the bean field on top to mark the spot, thus effectively scaring me out of one play area.

During the late Spitz years, he shared the limelight with Kaiser, who pinned me to the couch, growling, and then got taken to the vet. Kaiser: the catalyst for my mom's desire to learn how to put animals to sleep.

After Kaiser, Ringo arrived. Nights before my dad drove to a neighboring town to pick up Ringo, excitement made it hard for me to sleep. Ringo was a sheep dog. Instinctively, she would herd the sheep! No longer would I have to walk into the stinky, dim barn, find the smooth wooden sheep cane and short whip and walk the pasture chasing the sheep home. Ringo, the black and white sheep dog would do it!!

Ringo had a fascination with stones in the driveway. She barked at them, she drooled on them, she ran in circles around them. The stones fascinated her so much she had no time for the sheep. My sister and I continued to search the pasture for the sheep, herd them home at dusk and then walk by Ringo barking in the driveway.

Barking at stones apparently stressed Ringo out. One evening she bit my dad in the butt. The next day, no Ringo.

After Ringo, came Katie, a wiggly black lab-shepherd cross who waited with her mouth open under the hayloft door for newborn kittens, their eyes still closed, to fall down. When she started eating the ducks and geese also, she disappeared.

Then came Cricket, a short fat some-kind-of dog from the pound. After Spitz, Kaiser, Ringo, and Katie all left the family, someone made the economic and reality driven decision to get dogs from the pound instead of paying for a dog with a known family.

Not having a dog was not an option. True farms had dogs. Our farm, though we had little tractors and not much land, was a real farm. And we had a dog to prove it.

Cricket farmed with us for a decent amount of time. However, during the season we dressed the geese out, she snacked on goose bones which expanded in her intestines, killing her. After Cricket, Freckles took up residence in the doghouse.

My mom picked Freckles, a hyper-active poodle mixed with something. In addition to getting dogs without families, my mom also ruled out big dogs. Only little dogs, but not inside. She may have learned how to put animals to sleep, but she still clung to the city part of her that believed her house would not have animals in it.

The cats stayed outside, the dogs stayed outside, the lambs that got left by their mothers in the pasture got brought into the kitchen and placed in a cardboard box padded with straw. My mom sat next to them for hours, using a blow dryer to warm them. Sometimes I held the blow-dryer, but mostly she moved it slowly up and down the length of the shivering carcasses. My dad found the lost lambs and brought them to her to save.

```
Dear Angela,
     Our bell system at school consists of one
child holding a piece of metal and striking
another piece of metal that hangs from the tree.
The bell boy has much status.
```

When Charles visited me the first time, it created a mini carnival. I, and everyone in the village, suspected that *Monsieur Yovo* did not arrive at my house to talk about missing snow or the upcoming elections. Charles wanted booty.

Leaning against a wall at my first Peace Corps party, I had listened while other volunteers dissected PC relationships. In the land of malaria and voodoo, being "in love" required too much effort. Most relationships existed because of hormones.

Not mine. Charles: cute brown eyes, curly hair, nice shoulders, polished kisses. He spoke French and searched out adventure. He had deferred graduate school to volunteer in Africa. The object of my love more than any of the farm boys I had dated in America, potentially Charles was "the one."

However, the villagers understood that Charles had an objective. Maybe his one ambition showed in his rapid walk from his taxi to my house or maybe not taking a real shower for months made his pheromones stronger. Maybe I smiled too much when I saw him, but as soon as Charles in his pitted out plaid seersucker shirt, mango stained khakis, and sweat rag in one hand had taken one step past the concession gate, Big Mama, on her back on her straw mat, let laughter ripple her belly. Papa Rachidi looked at Charles, looked at me looking at Charles, and announced to the whole concession that tomorrow *Madame Yovo* would be tired.

Ikilou and Wilfried had been at the *marché* when Charles' taxi arrived. They stood next to him, each carrying one strap of his bag, smirking. Big Mama stopped laughing. In Fon she started reciting prayers. She paused to tell me that she planned to pray fervently that I would figure out how things were supposed to be done in that big bed I had. Most of the villagers didn't have beds, but they had kids. I didn't.

Charles and I went inside. Big Mama, Papa Rachidi, Ikilou, Wilfried, Rachidi, Akala, and several other students who had followed Charles from the main road where the taxi had dropped him off stood around my door, smiling as I shut it.

Charles hadn't shaved in at least a week, he smelled faintly of goat piss, and a crowd of people stood six feet away waiting for him to give me babies. It killed my sex drive. I kicked his bag away from the door, rolled out the straw mat for him to sit on, and gave him a cup of water. After twenty minutes of silence, I told him we could go out.

Later that night, when I thought we didn't have an audience, I helped him wipe his first layer of dirt off with a personalized bucket shower. Then we came up with many sweaty and creative ways to dissolve loneliness.

I loved that weekend. The next week, he sent letters full of "sweetie" and "can't wait to see you." Our relationship was based on our mutual desire to learn and our passion for writing.

Beaker didn't think so. She labeled us a typical PC couple, pointing out Charles endured public hand-holding, never verbally agreed with the repeated statements that he was indeed fortunate to have a woman like me. I noticed at night, pauses appeared after my question, "Aren't you glad to be with me?" Time spent out of bed or in conversation grew shorter.

Still, I had faith. Beaker didn't. She hinted that since Charles believed volunteers represented the American ideal, he felt pressured to pretend to be in love in order to maintain prestige in front of the villagers. He didn't want anyone to label us lonely, frustrated young people shacking up. Possibly, when we met other "couples" in the capital, he still pretended to be in love because it elevated himself above the others.

I countered her claims. Charles cared about me. He planned to be a lawyer; he based his life on logic. Logically, in this strenuous environment, it was safer to hide emotions.

I tried to placate mine also. I never admitted I wanted him to surprise me by renting a bush taxi and making the six-hour trip from his village to mine so we could commiserate about the lack of Oreos every weekend. Once he had taken me out for bush rat and warm beer. One other time he bought me a Snickers bar when we were in the capital. He had seemed extremely proud of his generosity and spontaneity. But he was too frugal to haggle with a bush taxi driver and sweat for six hours in a stinky car just to see me every five days. Still, I ached for his arrival. Each night before I fell asleep, I told myself that I could handle the absurdity of teaching English to African villagers who would benefit from it just as much as if I taught them how to ice skate by reminding myself that I was in love. I had found a really terrific guy.

Charles didn't visit the next weekend, and, in order to maintain our relationship, I started making plans to journey to his village. Peace Corps romance was all about adventure, but I was exhausted. Not to mention I had no money for a bush taxi since I'd spent a lot on cloth at the *marché*. When I said I wanted to leave, Big Mama cautioned me about the dangers related to leaving. I wrote Charles with a legitimate explanation about why, though I truly missed him, I had stayed in Glazoué.

According to Big Mama, driving tempted the gods to take your life. Though she never traveled, she spoke as an expert on the dangerous un-paved roads filled with pot-holes, the high-speed taxi crashes, and the exorbitant cost of finding a safe taxi. I let myself get caught up in her horrifying stories: eight school kids killed when their taxi rolled on Tuesday going from Abomey to Dogbo, one taxi exploded at the Azuvé taxi station due to bad wiring, and in Charles' village, a drunk taxi driver ran into a tree. Her last story, a sure sign to stay at home.

VENTRILOQUISTS
A palm—tappity, tap, tap—on bongos
in a tin shed moves the women waving scarves
and no one speaks because the women can't,
when facing the Catholic priest, start to talk
of dying babies, being starved of food

by wife number three. So the drums become
their voice. Tap right foot, stamp left, use the pain
to throw the arms up, face towards heaven—God
is fooled. Before his Book and Altar come
the women, praying, having lost their faith.

Because Big Mama and Mama Rita decided that the way to
keep me in Glazoué was to ask the God I knew to intervene,
Akala took me to the Christian Church: three hours in a tin
shed surrounded by banana and palm trees, trying to convince
myself that a tin roof was not a good conductor of heat.

To fix in our hearts	*Outside beauty roams.*
we repeat the Lord's Word,	*Raw wind completes*
Psalm 119: 105	*the sun. I could never*
"Your word is a lamp	*deny loving*
Unto my feet and a	*nature, or say I wasn't*
Light unto my path.	*excited by stars hovering*
Your word is a lamp	*at night amidst heat,*
Unto my feet and a	*stares, and bamboo whacks*
Light unto my path.	*falling on Afi's legs.*
Your word is a lamp	*I'm 22, saving*
Unto my feet and a	*the world*
Light unto my path".	*and myself.*
Sing to our Lord!! [1]	*I'm scared.*
Dance to the Altar,	
Not with the joy of whiskey,	*Oh God, if I*
But with the Joy of our Lord!	*have to dance*
Dance! Hallelujah! Give!	*up to the altar,*
Amen! White girl—Dance!	*let there be whiskey.*
God will hear your prayers!	*Shit.*

The idea of praying sometimes made me queasy. My Mennonite father prayed because in France, my inner warrior goddess discovered I had legs. And I liked them. So did the boys.

At one time my father liked legs also. At first, I only suspected that my father once liked legs, but later my mother confirmed my suspicion. My Mennonite father had not always been *Mennonite.* He had stories too. They weren't lost. They were smothered when he decided to be Thoreau, leaving academia, packing us in the cab of his pickup and moving back to his father's farm so he could raise his family to appreciate simplicity and God.

Too busy trying to farm and survive the economic crisis of the eighties, my mother never talked about our life before simplicity. My father started teaching again, this time high school, to keep the sheep. Through near bankruptcy and firing from the teaching job, they were the "people" with whom he talked. His sheep: his friends.

My mother went to garage sales. As our contribution to saving the family, my sister and I started earnestly working the land with my father. I had not read Thoreau, but I cursed whatever had put us on the farm.

I sang to the stars and packed my backpack with a radio and a blanket and ran away. I left after school one day and started to follow the railroad tracks out of town. I wanted my elementary school boyfriend to come with me. He told his mom who called the substitute teacher and the cops. Within an hour, a cop car pulled up next to me and my bright orange backpack and convinced me to go to my grandparents' house where my mother picked me up and took me home to get spanked.

Midnight. I sang "Amazing Grace" to my dad's favorite brand of sheep: Montadales. I tilted my head back so the stars shone directly into my eyes and down my throat— reaching my soul and stopping the turmoil. But they never did. I sang and sang and sang, waiting for angels, listening to the rustle of cornstalks, anticipating winged calmness that never came. The bank and the church could save us. My father believed. Saving money, saving souls. Plowing fields, passing the offering plate. He boasted that stacking straw bales, castrating sheep, and cutting lamb tails comprised my most refined skills. I would have flunked every *Glamour* magazine quiz on twenty ways to look sexy. My muscle strength, strong respect for my physical environment, and agility at getting out of the way of a stampede of sheep shaped a peculiar femininity, which somehow seemed to fit more in this African village than it did in the States.

I worked alongside my father in the dust of sheep lots, dodged the strings of cuss words during de-worming and no longer noticed the smell of singed flesh when burning lamb tails. My grandfather watched my sister and me heft alfalfa bales into sheep feeders and thought, "This is the beginning of good." Like many of the villagers here, I knew importance lay in the survival of the animals and crops.

In college I discarded the Mennonite German and music for French and theater. I started kissing boys, at first only on stage and then on actual dates. With pierced ears and cleavage shirts I waxed *moderne*. Yet, in France as in America, the boys could still tell I had been brought up on a strict diet of corn and church and work.

Back on the farm with mini skirts and make-up, I quieted the urge to run away again. Instead I read: Maya Angelou. Carolyn Forche. Thoreau. Sharon Olds. Martin Luther King. And Thoreau again. I thought I understood my father. Under the Parisian designer dress my soul nudged me. It coursed under my freckled skin wanting to posses the vibrancy of wind and tears, loneliness and stars, all escaping through a smile.

I cried in the sunshine and laughed at letters from home to hear only my responding echo. But I also danced naked under the moon in November with the bats and mosquitoes. And I learned about words; their power, their passion, their necessity. I wrote—urgently, letters, poems. I needed to connect two worlds, to redefine beauty. Language became my power, my privilege.

The villagers called me *yovo,* teecha, *madame, mademoiselle,* sister. My letters spoke of the desperate, the vibrant, the hagglers, the mamas. I created them. They created me. My language labeled, defined them. Did I have the right to do that?

Voodoo stalked the villagers, sequestering me. Ceremonies, curses, good luck, bad. In whispers. In conversations that ended when I walked by. Big Mama held her silences as I held mine, for protection.

Dear Angela,
My original goal for my classes centered on teaching English. Now I consider a successful class one in which all machetes remain on the floor.

When I first arrived in Benin, a seasoned volunteer asked me what music I had packed. My listening library consisted of a short-wave radio and a few dubbed tapes.

Seeing this situation as an opportunity to befriend an American male and also exchange tapes, I offered to swap mine for his, temporarily. He confidently explained he had no music to swap. He had planned to drum on his chest and sing with the locals.

Before leaving the States, he must have read the same books that I had about volunteers having calm, quiet, profound moments while becoming integrated into the local culture. Someday I wanted to meet those people, and Thoreau, to learn the exact definitions of their "calm, quiet, profound moments."

They obviously were using a dictionary vastly different from mine.

As the months passed, Beaker and I wrote many letters to each other comparing experiences, cataloging complaints, and encouraging one another. In one, she said Afi had come to see her because the brother of one of Afi's friends always beat her friend for bad grades in English. The girl, of course, did not have an English book, making it hard to study. Beaker wanted to know if I had an extra book.

Afi's friend, probably the 204th person to ask me for an English book and probably the 345th girl I knew who had been beaten for bad grades, personified my dilemma. I had bought two books for Akala and Pelagie, the girls who helped with my laundry and brought me water, on their promise to tell no one. However, gleaming new English books coddled by girls who do laundry, specifically the laundry of the new *yovo* English teacher, were easily traceable. Students followed me on my bike, tailed me in the *marché*, brought me bags of mangoes, offered to sweep my house, all in exchange for a textbook. I couldn't finance it.

At first when Beaker wrote me to say she had rented an apartment in her village for Afi and another student, I suspected a scam. I feared Beaker had crossed the line between constructive volunteering and sentimental involvement with the local population. Afi's father disapproved of her living outside of her village and attending school. When he withdrew payment for her fees, Beaker stepped in to ensure that Afi could stay in school.

Danger lay in overriding his decision. In the villages, women, even foreign women, dared not challenge a man's decision. It vaguely reminded me of home. However, Beaker and I had started learning an important lesson: giving halfway was not an option here. Once involved, we became hopelessly entangled, almost handing over all of our selves, physically, emotionally, and financially.

Beaker assured me that Afi genuinely wanted to learn and truly appreciated the help. I realized that Beaker, like me, was lonely and I assumed she had taken to mothering a student whose true desires were monetary, a pitfall all too common among PCVs.

Shortly thereafter, I visited Beaker in her village. On the map Dogbo appeared to be a two-hour journey. I re-calculated the trip in African time and figured five. On that basis I left my house at seven a.m., hoping to arrive by noon.

The first bush taxi rocketed past me on the spottily paved road, squealed to a stop, then reversed. Squinting at me, the driver made it clear he wanted no *yovos* as passengers, but, he condescendingly offered me a ride—for double the price. I answered with a haughty shake of my head. Another passenger, riding in the bitch seat with the stick shift between his legs berated the driver so lustily that he finally consented to take me for the standard fare.

As we jostled and jolted along, I contented myself by making a mental tally of the albino babies seen through the dusty windows of the taxi. Upon reaching Bohicon, I sought yet another taxi for the short ride to Abomey from where I would engage a third taxi to Azuvé and finally a fourth to Dogbo.

Since no taxis heading to Abomey were full, I selected the least dilapidated of the lot, claimed a seat and settled in to wait for it to fill. And I waited. Ignoring vendors selling toothbrushes, oranges, Kleenex and bread, I dozed in the heat. One man approaching the taxi, stopped, stared, and with one smooth movement swung a large wooden crate through the open door onto my lap, yelling, "You buy!" at the same time flipping the lid open to reveal a live baby crocodile.

I heaved and suppressed the vomit reflex. On a band trip to Florida in the eighth grade, I had developed an unreasonable fear of alligators after visiting a "live and in the wild" exhibit of alligators. Death in the jaws of an ancient alligator recurred in my nightmares.

Paralyzed by the fear of toppling the crocodile onto my lap and thus materializing my nightmare, I gasped. With the true ardor of a salesman, he began his litany on the virtues of crocodiles in houses. Making a deliberate effort to exhale, I emphatically explained that I couldn't buy the crocodile because it didn't have a name. And with that, I locked my eyes on his and gave the crate a shove. He blinked, squinted, picked up his crate and walked away.

All during this non-transaction the bush taxi had been slowly filling with passengers and with passengers' animals. The driver, having finished his flirtations with the girl selling bananas, sauntered over, felt under his seat, extracted the nails necessary to keep the doors shut and with a hammer sealed us in for the trip. We were off!

My mantra, "just because it's not America doesn't mean it's bad" got me through the ride to Abomey, and the hour wait for a taxi to Azuvé. However, it failed me completely when the engine of the bush taxi to Azuvé erupted in flames. I grabbed my bags and ran. When I finally did arrive in Dogbo, aboard a taxi that had been hot-wired by its resourceful driver, Beaker welcomed me with the much loved arrival beer and her much loved "daughter."

Afi truly was a rarity among my experiences in Benin. She laughed. While I recognized the obvious differences between American kids and the kids I taught in Benin—uniforms, language, gestures—I had not yet noticed all of the subtleties, especially the lack of laughing and smiling, until I met Afi. Her laughter and spontaneity caught me off guard, washed up memories, and made me instantly homesick. For some reason she hadn't given up or been beaten down. She had hope. She had that smile.

After spending a weekend in Beaker's house with Afi dropping in for visits, I felt what Beaker had found: a vibrant soul, a kindred spirit, a fourteen year old with a massive heart. Afi was the Peace Corps poster child, the one used in recruiting ads. Afi became the reason to stay in Benin and the subject of much of my writing.

Most volunteers quickly realized that effecting major changes in village patterns was not only exhausting and sometimes dangerous, but for the most part futile. Generally, PCVs found an "Afi" or two to focus on. For me, it was Akala and Pelagie, my water girls. They carried water and helped me with laundry. In return, I paid them with candy from care packages, school books and tutoring.

However, their helpfulness was conditional. Their initiative was usually determined by their lack of gum or the sight of me biking back from the post office with a large yellow padded envelope. Then after a polite five minute wait, I heard flip-flops hustle across the concession followed by clapping at the door. Akala and Pelagie had thought I might need water.

Two nights a week after dark and after they finished helping their moms, I tutored them. Each arrived with her own chair for sitting. My two chairs were placed with their backs to the wall to be used as desks. Setting candles on the corners of the "desks," I helped the girls read magazine articles aloud, take English dictation, and complete grammar exercises.

Sometimes I wasn't in the mood to teach English at night, or Akala and Pelagie were frazzled from early rising to gather wood and haul water, from attending school and going to the *marché,* from hauling more water and helping their moms cook. On those nights we put all the candles on one chair and sang and danced, encircling it. I taught them, softly, "Cecilia, "If I Had a Hammer," "Hark! the Herald Angels Sing," and my favorite from junior high, a spiritual, "light a candle." As we circled the chair, they helped me with my booty shakin', an art that I never completely mastered, but I did learn that feeling inept meant I was progressing. We swallowed our laughter because the grownups outside did not equate dancing and laughing with tutoring, and the girls would have quickly been called home to work.

When PCVs gathered and bitched about the bush taxis, the dysentery, the unidentified bug bites, the lack of chocolate and the days remaining of their service, they never mentioned their girls. It was dangerous to care so intensely about someone. Like the Africans who believed that the mere mention of a person's name, or the pointing of a finger at someone would attract evil spirits, the volunteers never spoke about their girls and their hopes for the girls' future.

I never said that I loved Akala and Pelagie because it was safe. I loved them because nothing else in my environment wanted my love, because I wanted someone to love me. I protected them as I needed to be protected. I told the professors at school that my girls couldn't go with them for study sessions under the mango trees. I told their mothers that they couldn't slap them when they burned cassava. I told the girls to come to my house, often. They were the reason that sometimes, for milliseconds, I considered staying in Africa forever...for milliseconds. I knew that I would cry for Akala and Pelagie when I finally boarded the plane for home.

I escaped the barrage of sexual advances, the eternal heat, the never ending screams of beaten children, the polio beggars, the AIDS victims, the women with clits sewn shut, the husbandless woman with three children and no food. I escaped all that by buying my two girls pencils, by telling them education was important. Sequestering them in my house, I talked and talked and talked about equality, about independence, about self-worth, about goals. Any change coming to Glazoué would start by my pouring love into these two girls. From the States my dad's church sent money that I passed on to the girls in the form of scholarships to ensure their continued education. On Peace Corps sponsored weekends, I packed them up and traveled to Cotonou, the capital. Whatever I could do to give value to my physical and emotional situation, I did. I desperately needed to believe that I was making a difference in the lives of these two children. This was to be "the toughest job I would ever love."

When PC sponsored Take Our Daughters to Work, a weekend in Cotonou, I took Akala and Pelagie, and they met Afi and smiled in public. The girls had never been in a bush taxi or a hotel, never seen electricity, toilets, Western food, telephones, typewriters and staplers. Akala, Pelagie, and Afi smiled and blinked and stared and smiled and just flat out gawked. Watching them interact over refrigerated, bottled sodas, made me think that they almost had reached the level of carefree. For an entire weekend they were surrounded by women who worked outside the home, who had formal educations, who encouraged them. And they were well fed, clean and cool. Finally, after nearly a year of service, I felt success.

Pelagie fell in love with the stapler. The first thing that she described when we returned home was not the television or the air-conditioned offices but the stapler. Later she remembered she had shadowed a nurse in a hospital and with a microphone given a speech in front of the other village girls and Peace Corps officials. And then she mentioned toilet paper. Her excitement echoed mine on one of my first solo ventures off the farm: Omaha, my aunt's big city big house and the Hot Dog Children's Theater. I was awestruck.

Dear Angela,
    If my neighborhood had a zip code, it would be 90210. I've got doors, screens, a private latrine, and a bike.

A cockroach's run to my kitchen or a frog's splash in the swamp proved silence didn't exist. Silence was just a degree of noise.

Days became bookended by the sun. Sunsets nurtured with

the haze sprouting from Big Mama's cook fire pulled me through the slow hours of dark measured by the slip of candle wax to awaken again to the un-civilized sound of saber-like palm fronds caressing one another beneath ominous cloud clusters melting across the sunrise.

I had thrown myself at life, not merged with it. Bruises. Lacerations. Battle scars. Proof. I wanted to become a woman.

Time here allowed me to understand and welcome the stillness felt by sensations that sat on the rim of my pores before slipping inside and joining the flow of cells to settle in my marrow.

Beaker told me blood was made up of hemoglobin and platelets and water. However, mine filled with the span of bat wings, the suave manner of roosters, the *légère* chirp of tree frogs in the dark.

Waves of color enriched the air. Flashes of color in Glazoué wrapped themselves around hips and over the curves of strong shoulders, covering heads that had eyes that didn't smile which protected hearts that did.

Papa Ikilou drummed, and the women and their multi-colored *pagnes* flowed past me: colors birthed from an unknown womb, pushed out strong. They bonded to cotton fibers, vibrated to the rhythm of the hands that stroked the taut goatskin that once covered the muscle and sinew of the animal that had found the source of life in clumps of grass and clusters of puddles supported by the layers of dirt covering the interior heat of the earth. Somewhere in those depths resonated the secret of "woman." I heard it. I didn't understand it.

Big Mama and Mama Inez walked as if the earth pushed their shoulders up, and the wind walked with them. Their dances mesmerized me. My mother had gone to dances; rather, she had gone to formals. Her gowns hid her hips. I had dreamed of wearing those gowns. In old photos I saw those dancing couples, but they were not talking with the world. My own dancing made my neighbors laugh. It didn't explain my searching. It didn't call the spirits. Secretly, I wanted to dance like Big Mama.

At high school dances I rarely left my chair next to the drinking fountain. I had no résumé to qualify me for this African movement. Big Mama's dancing called attention to the curves of form and invited rhythm to sustain the senses. Women's stories were told from the lift of the sole to its flat-slap against the earth. Their movements called to something, and the something heard and arrived and gathered, awakening energy. I didn't know the call. Before I arrived, I didn't know it existed.

Sometimes Big Mama sang: a full-bodied dusky voice enveloped her more than the smoke from her smoldering cooking wood. Sharing sorrow or mellowed beauty, a bit worn. Singing, stirring to the backdrop of women pounding *pilee*— the female drumming of the village.

Once I saw her walk up the path, flanked on both sides by the tall green grass, someone's baby secured to her chest with a red *pagne*. If Amazons had existed here, she would have been the queen.

With the wind the ex-sorority president stood
next to an empty corn crib, wire,
not the tall phallic kind—
the short, fat phallic kind.
In her frosted white cat glasses,
matching bag and heels,
she would have tripped over sheep turds.
She cried into crying. She wanted
to scream, but sound carried on the prairie.
The house was close. Sound carried.

His church didn't warm up to them,
the Mennonite who married
a non-Mennonite and then moved
back to Mennonite farm land.

She wrote home telling how he
trained their blond haired daughters
to castrate sheep and swing open
the white wooden door to their house
with a 12 gauge leveled
at the men.

The younger daughter, twenty,
a bar, southern France,
a dance floor, a ski instructor.

She thought she was a woman
when he took her shirt off and she danced.

Dear Angela,
    Appreciate your pre-packaged food! Monique's guide to successful fresh coconut acquisition and eating:
    1. Climb coconut tree
    2. In the process of starting to climb, discover that you do not have the appropriate leg muscles to power yourself up the tree
    3. Find a small child and request that he climb the tree and get coconut
    4. Find a large, very large, could-probably-kill-a-hippo, knife

5. Remember how you sliced your finger, not the tomato, in Home Economics class
6. Decline to use the very large hippo-killing-knife to crack the coconut held between your feet
7. Seek out a local to crack the coconut between his feet
8. Drink the coconut milk and dig out the meat
9. Decide that coconuts are not vital to life

Her book and her butt on the cement,
Pelagie learns English, a language as foreign
as the concept of curling up in a chair
to read. The lantern lights the words
and beckons the mosquitoes
who add bites next to the bruises
given to her by her father before
he gave her the order to sweep the sand
and wipe his moto while he donned his beret
and khakis and then rumbled off to protect
his wallet with the 100 and 200 franc pieces
that slid into his dusty palm as taxis without papers,
door-handles, ignitions, or windshields
shimmered past him along the one paved road.

He smiled, shook my hand, and politely
averted his eyes. "Beninese mirages,"
he said. "You must have seen a mirage.
Only taxis with papers pass by me."

Back against rubber, feet sprawled into nothingness, tail whipping, the lizard twisted in the slingshot. Outside Beaker's screen door, Afi aimed over the concession wall. With good aim, the lizard recovered from the flight and dumbly lumbered into the swamp. Poor aim bonded the lizard with the concrete in a way that left a lasting impression as the impact chipped paint, and the corpse flopped to the ground to be picked up and shot again until a mama's shouts snuffed Afi's giggles and scared her sweaty fingers into stillness.

BREAKFAST WITH CHARLES, BEACH WEEKEND
I read a book in jr. high
where a hurt girl swam
with dolphins and they healed her.

She danced, kissed a boy
and he kissed her back,
sand underneath her feet,
no concrete in sight. She biked
there with the sun
wrapped through the spokes.
She held onto her laughter
like handlebars and swam
'til the water angels came
and splashed and smiled velvet.
Their eyes cracked her soul.
The waves turned it into
sea glass.

This morning I awoke to only the sight of white
foam slamming the sand.

It doesn't know me,
this sea in which I can't swim.
You say neither do the stars
although I plastered myself
on gravel roads and sang to them,
admitted my heart wanted
to dance with tigers,
scratch the noses of hippos,
and back-float under a waterfall.
I knew that water would know me.
Falling from far above, it would
have talked with the stars.

An African moon three-quarters full awakens the blood in the fire-breathing-voodoo-god-lizard, Devi. I'll catch him, leash him, and train him. "Breathe!" and my rice will be cooked. "Breathe!" and the mice will be dead. "Breathe!" and candles will be lit. After I've lassoed him, he'll come to class with me—teacher's pet. "Breathe!" and all will be quiet. "Breathe!" and they will conjugate. "Breathe!" and they'll pick mangoes for me.

I set out two dead roaches on top of three squashed spiders, but I've not heard the scurry, not yet felt the heat from you, Devi. Why must you hide while I sit here alone, drinking? There's enough for you—I'd be a considerate captor, almost a friend. I'll wait, drinking 'til the moon has faded. Drinking 'til the *pastis* is gone. Drinking 'til in the slurred blink of my eye my ramblings convince me that you, reptile on the wall, breathe fire.

Dear Angela,
   Typical PCV profile: educated, bi-
lingual, well-traveled, savvy. We have good
conversations:
   PCV 1: Hey, how's it going?
   PCV 2: Not bad—You still got the shits?
   PCV 1: Yeah, but I haven't gone for 50
minutes.
   PCV 2: Wow. That's great! Mine is slowing
down as well. Last time I was in there for a
long time, but when I looked at it, it looked
more solid than this morning, so maybe my
parasites are dying off inside my intestines.

Under the dancing stars
the wind hugged my freckled legs,
imploring me to stay.
To them I had returned

this time knowing
to stand
tall and proud
and dance
with my shadow
and smile
alone
and love

myself.

Dear Angela,
    Fear I never had before: a cockroach bite on
my ass.

Days like today I miss you.
On a moto with a buzz
from a grand biere and a shot
of the carpenter's sodabei,
I ride and think how I'd like
to share the moment with you—
the people flashing through my visor,
the speed, the wind, the moving clouds—
I'd like you to feel the same, or to come home
to you and explain the reason for the buzz
and laugh and get you a drink
and continue the evening.

I was a second grader in the girls' bathroom with my short haircut. At home, we were on "the austerity program." My mom cut my hair, not Rachel at Kathy's Kut 'N Kurl, which is where Sarah, Renae, and Linda went. I was washing my hands when a third grader pointed at me and said, "Boys aren't supposed to be in the girls' bathroom."

My dad wanted sons. Maybe he didn't, but he should have had them. He wanted someone to want to farm with him. To feel the glow of the wheat fields, to talk with his sheep. He always talked with his sheep.

He worked us like boys. We planted, fenced, castrated, weaned, cultivated, baled, and harvested. Everyone knew the

Schmidt sisters worked like sons. Dad would pack a trailer tight with bales and then ride into town with the front seat of his pick-up full of his daughters, wondering to whom they would rent their inheritance.

At sunrise and sunset
in a slow row of six
we shuffle by you with basins
of water on our heads,
backs taut, eyes averted,
we sing to steady our steps:

Don't sit there white girl and bitch
about the heat.
We've never seen water on your head
or kids strapped to your back.
You stare and drink,
buy new shoes,
and go to the capital,
not to the well to get water.
Don't sit there white girl and bitch
about loneliness.
We've never seen you beaten by your man
after he's slept with someone else.
We see you at the post
counting your packages
then biking back to your house,
not to the well to get water.

Don't sit there white girl and bitch
with your hands folded in your lap
while Little Rita and Rachel shell peanuts
and Papa Roland leaves for the manioc fields.
You won't join our slow shuffle,
but you can't just bitch, white girl—

Look at Little Rita—
wearin' underwear and dirt,
dancin' for an orange
from you, she wants
an orange, white girl,
not English.

You want to live with us—
then show us your vibrance
shakin' your shoulders,
bendin' your backside.
White girl, get down—
your soul must command
the tam tam's rhythm.
Papa Roland has AIDS

And there's more dirt than water
in our well,
you understand?
If you're living with us,
show jubilation,
hear our drums—
prove you feel
the earth owns your spirit.

Swallow our palm wine,
sing with your laughter.
Rachel's got no kids,
this rainy season isn't wet,
but dance 'til you sweat
and mud forms between your toes.

No one understands
your formal French
or how you can teach
when you can't bargain for rice.
This village needs a pump,
but we got you.

I braved the bush taxis to visit Beaker. I arrived late, but Beaker remained nonplussed. We had stopped writing—"I'll see you around four." And started writing, "I'm aiming for sometime late Friday. If I'm not there by four on Saturday, it means something happened and I'm not coming."

Beaker stunned me this visit. She had no welcome *biere* on hand and absolutely no food in the house. Having no food did not surprise me. Volunteers, not having refrigerators, and the villages not having convenience stores, rarely had food or snacks. The exception being when angels of some sort had free time to personally watch over the transport of our care packages and help them securely pass through customs, get loaded on a mail truck, appear mundane to our local post-office personnel and, therefore, miraculously arrive at houses, full of melted chocolate and bars of soap, both of which, during the two or three weeks it had taken to cross the world, had started taking on characteristics of each other, making enjoying them a rather bizarre experience, but a delight nonetheless.

Care packages showed a volunteer's soul. Some volunteers shared the Oreos and let others read their *New York Times*. Some volunteers didn't. Some volunteers hovered as the recipient tore open the puffy yellow envelope. Others asked to be given chunks of almond toffee and wanted to know when they could use the watermelon shower gel.

Beaker had not gotten any care packages recently. While I had left Glazoué extremely excited to see her, I was also hoping she might have some licorice or chocolate. One time, someone had sent her brownies. After six hours in a bush taxi, I felt as if the sand had clawed its way through my skin to coagulate in my bloodstream. Lethargy, heat, dehydration. A godsend that she had no *biere*. I rehydrated, downing several Nalgene bottles. Water filled my stomach, and it remembered it contained nothing but water. Not having American *bon choses,* we grabbed flashlights and left her compound to search out some fried cassava and, since I had rehydrated, several grand *bieres*.

The *teinti* who usually sold us *biere* had a problem with her generator, thus no beer. A full moon had stationed itself above us, and the lizards ran from the branches of mango trees to the roofs of houses; we continued our walk. At the second *buvette,* a large group of men sat around: free *bieres,* but also hassle over the whereabouts of our husbands.

After walking about five kilometers we finally found our food and beverage for the night at the *buvette Dieu Seul Sait* with friendly mamas who refilled our fried cassava supply with the hottest and freshest as soon as it was finished. We chatted with them, talked about how hard it was to live without our husbands, explained that my freckles were not a skin disease.

Eventually, *Dieu Seul Sait* closed. We shuffled our sandals in the sand and giggled. The walk didn't seem as long this time. Halfway back, Beaker discovered she didn't have her keys. No care packages and now no keys. Exhaustion from the ride and the *bieres* hit me. I told her I would just wait for her at this spot. She left. And not only exhaustion hit, the three Grand Flags that I drank wanted out of my bladder. I now knew not to mess around with my bladder. But I was too far from *Dieu Seul Sait* to go back and see if they had a latrine, and still too far from Beaker's house. Plus, if Beaker returned from the *buvette* and could not find me, the "mad" part of her nickname would rear itself, and she was liable to start a small war demanding to know who had kidnapped me, probably turning me into a zombie as she spoke.

About twenty-five feet from where I stood, there was a tree. I hadn't been very good at squatting when I entered the country, but my bathroom skills had flourished here. My ability to squat and aim filled me with a bizarre pride, and I never ceased to marvel at the variety of places available for relief.

When we had gone up north for our "safari," I had initiated the contest to see if we could fill an elephant's footprint. The ground had been so dry we had not succeeded, though we had lined up fairly close to one another and tried to immediately position ourselves over the print. I had not foreseen Peace Corps building that kind of teamwork, nor self-esteem.

The tree presented an easy pee, a three out of ten. Maybe a four because it was right next to the road, but the full moon was now directly above it; so it created some shadow underneath. I could go under there without the risk of what volunteers called the "glow-butt" effect. Under a full moon, without cover, the white volunteers positively shone. Embarrassing or entertaining, depending on one's perspective.

I smartly walked over, gathered my skirt, squatted. The welcome sound of sand being dampened at close range. I sighed, then stiffened. Due to the strength of the urge, I had not carefully surveyed my surroundings. Three Beninese slowly walked down the path in front of me. I hoped the shadow of the tree would save me, along with the fact they were also shuffling through the sand on their way home from a *buvette*.

"*Yovo*, what are you doing under that tree at 1:30 in the morning?"

Shit. I stopped myself midstream. I tried to stand up, letting the front of my dress fall down first, then tugging the back into position, still semi-squatting, "I'm waiting for a friend."

"It's very dangerous to wait for a friend under a tree at this time of night." They thoroughly enjoyed talking to the *yovo* and stayed. I prayed and tightened. Minutes later, Beaker arrived with her keys. She asked, "Why are you hunched up under the tree? Since when are you scared of talking with the Beninese?"

"Glow butt. I was trying to avoid the glow butt phenom when they sauntered by."

She chortled; I snorted. It put my muscles over the edge. I peed. Beaker doubled over. The Beninese looked at us, slapped their thighs in delight, and moved on under the light of the moon.

Dear Angela,
    I still love nature, but now I understand
what it takes to live intimately with her.

Somewhere under the new moon, worn palms
start the drumming, fetishers run by,
reeds scrape midnight into my wall.

On the surface of a bucket of water
I search for the flash of my smile,
anticipating the day
when in a tiled bathroom
a glance in a mirror will produce
only a thought of me
shivering in the dark.

Months of adventure
survived with daydreams
of memories.

At night I fall asleep
knowing Africa
has won.

Where do I go
when I dream?
Painful to awake

and remember I liked
being Daddy's little girl.

3

Eighteen Harvest Moons

COTONOU TO GLAZOUÉ
There were no signs for the speed limit of the slightly insane.

Windows down dust in the lungs—
my ears burned,
redness this time not caused by the sun.

Four hours in a five seater with nine others.

My bellybutton occupied itself twirling
around the fatigue entrenched
also in my eyebrows,
rubbed into the cuticles of my toes.

bumps

"and what are shocks?"
asked the driver
his right hand reaching between
the khaki cotton of another man's legs
to shift.
The rusted metal frame dry heaved forward—
total windburn-on-the-cheek gear.

Next to me a man slapped his goat.
It peed on my bag.

I had what we call luck—

the cookies that had taken a month to reach me
snarfed up the piss before it blurred my letters.

Over the motor I heard laughter.
"It's not like this where you're from,
is it?"

My stomach tried to strangle my small intestines
by wrapping itself around and around them.

Little Rita waited for me, her hair in spiked braids—
a last lost stegosaurus.

Her diet of rice and oil could not nourish a dinosaur.

During the month for bananas, I saw
her bug bitten hands hold the treat.

Her poochy tummy smiled, size four

calloused feet tapping contentment
in her mama's store.

Often, mama watched the bush taxis
arrive then depart, sold nothing
and yelled at the women selling bananas.

TAXIS (to be remembered to avoid rip-offs)
Glazoué to Dassa	400 francs
Glazoué to Savé	300 or 400
Glazoué to Bohicon	1200
Dassa to Bohicon	800 (they always say 1000, but only *yovos* pay that)
Bohicon to Abomey	150 or 300 with zemijahn
Abomey to Azuvé	800
Azuvé to Dogbo	300
Glazoué to Cotonou	2500 (Petit Fils has the fastest taxi)
Glazoué to Tchararou	1600

```
Dear Angela,
    Things I am thankful for (In honor of
Thanksgiving and David Letterman)
    8. I have discovered no green mambas in my
bed.
    7. I have not had to leave my classroom for
an uncontrolled dash to the latrine.
    6. The machetes kids bring to school are not
used on teachers.
```

5. Voice of America may be cheesy, but at least it's news.
4. Roosters in Glazoué don't start crowing until 4:30 a.m.
3. I have not seen any crocodiles in the swampish area behind my house.
2. I have not eaten rat/dog or other unknown animals for over a month.
1. I am thankful for people who write me letters and send packages!!

IKILOU
Unaware the world is round
but knowing pythons are gods,
he goes to church,

dances, gives francs.
Then Jesus, the mayor, teachers
and neighbors see he is civilized

thus can be saved.
Hallelujah, Hallelujah, Jesus
Praise God all day.

At night, slide the knife
through the brown cheek flesh,
once on the left,

once on the right,
so the spirits of the cough
and hot skin that killed Papa will see

there is respect for them even though
every Sunday on the wooden bench
under the tin roof he sits

listening to the stories
of David and Goliath and Samson,
watching the minister in his robes

as he collects the offering,
prays for salvation,
and finally leaves

them both wondering,
what if Jesus were to wrestle the python?

LINGUISTIC COMPETENCE II

Choose the correct comparative/superlative. (2 pts.)

1. Charles got a 14 in math. Kyle got a 12 in math. Charles is (worse, better, best).
2. Alex got a 9 in English. Angela got a 13 in English. Beaker got an 11 in English. Angela is the (worse, better, best).

Roosters crowed and school started at eight a.m. if it didn't rain. Little khaki clad monsters slapped their desks and stood.

"Good morning, teecha."

The wind warned of a storm. Ikilou said, "Teecha, please, no class today—bad spirits," then whispered, gesturing to show how I could die like his uncle—killed by falling thunder.

I paced, dripped sweat on their desks. "To sing—repeat after me—I sing, you sing, he/she/it sings."

Seventy students glad to escape the manioc fields repeated "I sing, you sing..." Wild goats wandered through the class shedding fleas and sleeping powder.

Unit Six in the French designed curriculum—the birthday unit. No one understood "cake" or "birthday party." Neither existed. The verb section began with a picture of a candle and the verb "to blow."

"Repeat after me—I blow, you blow, he/she/it blows." Seventy voices mimicked, "I blow, you blow..." In my mind, memories sprang up. "Past tense, repeat—I blew...."

The candle picture helped no one understand, so I *blew* the dust off the table. They handed in their homework—*My brother blew the mosquitoes. My sister sees flies and blows them.*

I decided not to teach them prepositions. I focused on pronunciation. "Class, repeat— teach errrr. Good morning, teacherrrrr." The chorus repeated "teechaa good morning teechaa."

In the dusty humidity I stuffed sweat into my backpack, cursed Ikilou who had run away after saying, "Madame, we understand teacherrrrr. That is not the problem. In some villages, teechaa means lobster."

MOVEMENT IN B FLAT

I.

My father's white Ford, cab packed
with four, slid up two states
to South Dakota. Between my

mother and her family, Nebraska—
between me and ballet, gymnastics,
softball, and basketball—
piano.

II.

I wanted to ride
our ponies. The colt wasn't broken
yet. Most of us weren't.

III.

My mother found a Czechoslovakian
refugee to instruct me. He had survived
whatever travesty had happened
to immigrate to South Dakota.
I never thought to ask why.

IV.

I rode the Allis Chalmers and kept my eyes
on the tree two miles away to drive
straight. The neighbors would
comment.

V.

Saturday mornings, my sister
and I yelled at each other as she drove
the forty-five minutes to his house where she
shoved me forward to knock until wafts
of his sausage breath opened his door.
Music had kept him alive.
When he cried, he played. When I played,
I cried.

VI.
Even a girl can.
Even a girl can.

VII.
He suggested
the first twenty times I practice
only the first two lines.

VIII.
I was going to be stunning.

IX.
I did not look at the piano twenty times
during the week. My sister, the musical
prodigy, played her piece and in
the kitchen, I heard his wife
sigh in relief.

A wrinkle in time—Madeleine L'Engle must have thought of Africa when she dreamed up that title. For a regional project I went to a remote village with a group of volunteers to work on a mapping project. The idea: village women would map out their village, drawing the places they frequented everyday or every week. We would analyze the map and, based on our conversations with them, determine the needs of the village, and where those needs, such as pumps, hospitals, etc. should be placed. Our goal centered on creating a low-cost, brilliant plan that the village could implement and use. This excursion ranked high on Peace Corps priorities. We used the Peace Corps SUV.

We rumbled into the village, laughing and looking out the amazingly clean glass windows as we slowly passed the mud huts with naked kids in the doorways. This village came closer to *National Geographic* than I thought possible. I dawdled in the car, the last volunteer out of the portable heaven. There weren't many opportunities to wage war on my heat rash, but when an opportunity drove by and picked me up, I did not want it to end sooner than necessary, even ten seconds sooner.

None of us spoke the local language, and the old, wrinkly, winnowy women didn't speak French. We found an interpreter. He explained what we explained: we wanted them to draw a map of their day-to-day activities in the village—where did they walk and for what reasons? Where and when was the *marché*? And the well? And where did they go if they were sick? And where were their town meetings?

We held our session with them under some trees, sitting on the ground. After the explanation, we set paper and pencil on the ground. No one picked up the pencil or moved to flatten out the brown paper that had immediately re-curled into its rolled shape. We asked the interpreter why the women did not start their map. He asked the women. They said they didn't understand.

One volunteer flattened out the paper and modeled the process. The women stared, unfamiliar with the pencil. After the volunteer passed the pencil to them, they held it as I had never seen a pencil held, with respect, a sharp contradiction to the crabby sentiments we had vocalized in the SUV about lack of easy access to the internet in the capital. We had entered a life where a pencil held importance. The women acknowledged and realized its power: a tool, a method of communication, a gift.

Slowly, deliberately, with intent, believing that the pencil would capture information, would make something permanent, would create history, would tell someone else about their lives and then their lives would become better, one woman made an X on the paper and said it was her house. With reverence, she gave the pencil to another woman who silently drew a slash and then another on top of it, saying that was her house. Each woman took a long time to put Xs where their houses were. Some small squabbles arose as to where some of them lived. None of the volunteers talked. Perhaps this was a *Peace Corps Moment*. In one second, we had just glimpsed how capitalistic and greedy and fast-paced our society could be. The village women, carefully passing the pencil from palm to palm, were teaching us something. It was possible we needed to learn this lesson more than my students needed to learn to conjugate, more than I needed to learn how to hand-wash my clothes, more than I needed to think about graduate school, more than I needed to check my mailbox when I got back to Glazoué and more than I needed to wonder if there would be pineapple at the *marché* on Wednesday. It was possible I needed to look at the pencil and understand the power of what I already had, had always had: the gift of communication. I had never thought to be thankful for a pencil. It was also possible I needed to be imbedded in the actual moment without the safety of jettisoning myself forward to my ideal future or backwards to the known past.

I thought I had been making a great sacrifice, living without, learning and sinking into village life, but I hadn't. Scared, I had kept my roots from wrapping around others' hearts, maintained a semi-permeable membrane between myself and village life. I had been overwhelmed by how much I could care about the village the minute I moved to Glazoué.

The pencil was held by wrinkled hands of women who spent time in the fields, hands wrinkled like the hands of my mother who didn't haul wood or work in the manioc fields but who left her elbow length gloves somewhere in Kansas and moved to South Dakota to drive a small Allis Chalmers into the prairie wind, who dug beets in our garden, who threw bales down from our hayloft, who had accepted a ring which had given her many other rings.

These women had hands like my mother. Hands that had

moments of silence, resting on top of a husband's hands, hands that crumpled clods of dirt in frustration, hands that recounted money searching for more, hands that knew life would not be understood or solved. Hands that had cooked large meals and wiped away tears.

I rubbed lotion on every day, but I wanted wrinkles like theirs: evidence of living. Their hands bragged they had not been kept indoors, manicured, as a trophy. Hands that let nature and life swarm over them, repeatedly. Hands that knew the risk of loving, but still did. These hands had faith in humanity. Hands that valued the chance to let someone else understand their lives, even if the understanding was limited to where their houses were in a small unheard of African village in a small unheard of African country.

I loved my mother. And I was far away from her. And I did not know why, but the way the woman in the green and yellow amoeba design *bomba* was gingerly, yet purposefully holding the pencil as she stroked two diagonal lines for the *marché* which occurred once a week, made me feel as if at least I was learning something.

Volunteers spent a lot of time thinking they "deserved" little treats because life was hard. And life was difficult, but by choice. We had chosen to be here because we wanted to help and to grow. But amongst the latrine battles and the discipline battles and the intestinal battles, the festivals, the grand *bieres,* and the loneliness, it was difficult to remember to learn, difficult to remain open enough to learn. It was hard to push aside the mosquito net every morning and slide into underwear, stiff and holey from the local soap and hand-washing, to reread letters from friends talking about email mishaps and jazz concerts, hard to walk down the hallway to greet the maggots, and say, "Wow! Today I'm going to have the opportunity to learn." I constantly searched for the mind tricks to turn it all into a sitcom, marveling at the fact I had to have so many coping mechanisms. I had thought I was invincible.

And when we sought out other *yovos* for companionship and buried ourselves in our picture books and letters, it became harder to notice the world around us and not the world we reconstructed as we wanted in our heads. America became a land full of happy, motivated, just, educated, stimulating people. Why had we left? Why did we stay, hot and frustrated? Sometimes our mentored girls reminded us why. But the pencil slammed into our psyches. Maybe we wanted too much. Maybe we already had a lot. Maybe what we owned, what we had lived, those we had loved, maybe the fact that we had multiple pencils back in our villages and could buy more if we wanted to, maybe that was enough.

Dear Angela,
    Today: 25 minutes spent looking at a picture of a chocolate cheesecake.

4

Fifteen Moons Full

COMPENSATION
The black man in blue
T-shirt and blue jeans
stood against a blue green sea
that used to support
slave ships hauling
his ancestors in shackles

and sweat to my country.
Should I wonder at his welcome,
sprayed with hostility and doubt
about my clear skin,
lighter than the sky his great, great grandfather
never saw on his journey

locked below,
skin pale as the shells
prickling his feet

on his native beach
where he fishes every morning
still reeling from my ancestors' sins.

I came as a volunteer
to teach his children English,
instill modern ideas about women,
introduce new methods of birth control,
nourish another generation
of slaves to the Western world.

LINGUISTIC COMPETENCE III.

Choose one of the words—who, which, that—and combine the two sentences into one sentence.

1. His brother now lives in Kilibo. He went to the university in Cotonou.
2. His wife works in the hospital. It is in Ouidah.

Correct the conditional sentences.

1. If I have money, I would buy a new bike at the market.
2. If he went to Kandi, he will speak Dendi.
3. If she is happy, she dance.
4. If Tano sells fans in the market, he has money.
5. If my brothers is hungry, they will eat pilee.

FAMILY REUNION
Once upon a time, she had a closet
full of gowns for balls.
On a trip to the big city
with a mall with 180 stores
plus a Dairy Queen and a Hardees,
I saw a yellow dress with ruffles
around the sleeves and the neck.
On the bottom, four rows of ruffles.
It was sixty dollars, expensive
for a woman who no longer wore
her gowns and instead ran around
a forty-acre pasture waving a wooden cane
in the air and yelling. Yelling to gather
the sheep. Yelling to make the flock
skedaddle home. Yelling
because late night discussions about dental
bills preceded the discussion
about the mirrors she installed downstairs
for her daughters.
My sister and I and our vanities.

For her family reunion, my yellow dress
with ruffles. Sixty dollars.
The price of a whole lamb
I was reminded.

My hair did not turn out for the photo anyway.

A moment of panic today. Big Mama asked me the name of
my husband. My mind became as empty as my latrine was full.
I rarely mentioned my husband any more. The laughter follow-

ing the villagers' questions let me know they didn't believe me. However, I never openly admitted I was single. My stories just became more confusing. Trying to derail the conversation, I mumbled something about his many studies and his increasing responsibilities with his aging mother.

Big Mama asked pointed, probing questions. Confusion wrapped itself around the village. I wore the wedding band, talked lovingly of Todd, and Mr. The Man Who Brought The Mail And Sometimes Kept It verified that I received letters addressed to "Madame." However, the villagers read body language enough to know something was up with Charles, and then there were all those male volunteers who still stopped by.

Last weekend, one came by my house, official reason—to check out the price of cashews in the Glazoué *marché*. Real reason—breaking up and delaying the eleven-hour ride up north to his village. We passed the days drinking warm beer and shining a flashlight down my latrine, trying to figure out what exactly squirmed down there. We had no success with our evaluation.

The rainy season had begun; so after emptying our first set of bottles, we slipped cautiously up the path from my house to the *buvette*. Arms outstretched, two empty beer bottles in each hand, we leapt from stone to stone across the swampy area in order to get new, full, warm bottles of beer. On the other side, still holding our arms out for balance, we stood on one leg to shake the microbe filled mud off our Tevas.

Papa Rachidi, returning from the *marché*, greeted the volunteer, and giving me a reproving glance, mentioned my husband. I planted my upraised sandal firmly on the ground, narrowed my eyes, flared my nostrils and proceeded to explain my husband's brother-in-law. This man, even though he looked like a scraggly, dirty, unshaven Peace Corps volunteer, was, in fact, my husband's brother-in-law.

Todd's mother had, unfortunately, taken a turn for the worse, and she needed him. Since the airline ticket was nonrefundable, his brother-in-law had stepped forward, out of familial obligation, to become my first visitor from the States. As long as I remembered that this PCV was now actually my husband's brother-in-law, I figured I would have no problems. To dodge Big Mama, I reminded her of my mother-in-law's health–always an important topic in the village–and diverted her attention from her original question. She asked me again to explain the specimen cups that cluttered my house. Shortly after I moved in, the first volunteers descended on my house—one planned, two due to bush taxi breakdowns, and one just wandering through—we called it my house warming. Out of politeness and curiosity, and to demonstrate to the other women that she had permission to walk into my house, Big Mama stopped by with some bananas for us.

The volunteers were flipping through my American photo book until the picture of the cheesecake served at my graduation party held them transfixed. Beaker gasped, pulled it from the album and said with reverence, "Cheesecake? You brought a picture of cheesecake with you to Africa?" The other three hunched around her. I told them that moments after that picture was taken, I had dumped the remainder of the cheesecake in the trash. Beaker stopped twirling her hair, "You threw it away?!"

In that moment of incredulity, Big Mama arrived with bananas. The wasted cheesecake distracted all of us; so she simply plopped her gift down on my table next to the anti-fungal cream and two stool samples that Beaker had promised to take to the medical unit for me. Big Mama picked up one of the small round bottles containing a semi-solid mustard colored lump; jokingly, she said she would take it to spice her *ignam pilee* sauce. Then she could see how *yovo* food tasted. We burst out laughing. Confused, she pointed out that she had just given us bananas; perhaps we could share with her in return.

I said it was my poop, repeating several times "my poop." Big Mama didn't understand 1) why I bottled my poop, 2) why the poop bottle sat on the table and 3) how I got the poop into the bottle. While grabbing both bottles from the table, along with the anti-fungal cream, I explained a bit about how the Peace Corps had a doctor who studied our poop when we felt sick and then gave us medicine. Big Mama "Hhhmphed," suggesting that I visit a fetisher, and then I wouldn't have to put poop in a bottle.

In America, I never entertained guests with specimen cups as table centerpieces. This time, it had not even occurred to me to remove them. In fact, I purposely set them on the table so that Beaker would remember to take them to the capital. A good friend transports your poop for free.

A good friend also hangs around a bit at a housewarming in Africa; the location itself giving a completely new significance to house "warming." This impromptu event started by sitting, just sitting and watching the sweat run down each other's face. Heat stifled the urge for beer, even a cold beer. After a long period of silence we did muster short verbal exchanges. Since we had been in country for months, we knew each other's life story. In the absence of TV, movies, malls, cruising, and phones, I suggested juggling onions. None of us could focus in the heat. The onions slipped out of our sweaty hands and rested on the dusty floor. Retrieval required too much energy. "Catch the Onion," once only one remained, had an entertainment value of three minutes.

```
Dear Editor:
    In your September Cosmo, you had an article
entitled "24 Ways to Feel Sexy." As part of the
24, your article listed
    1. Don't wear pantyhose.
    2. Turn off the lights and use only candles.
    3. Wear loose, flowing clothes.
```

I would like to tell you that those three suggestions make up my daily life, and I feel about as sexy as Jabba the Hut. Might I suggest you do further research and give your readers other ways to feel sexy because your current suggestions do not work.

Thank you.

Sincerely,
Monique Maria Schmidt

Afi told me
a bedtime story
of herself
as a child
with her mother:

a mother and child
child screamed
child screamed, "mother"
mother turned
mother pounded the manioc in the mortar
and turned to pound the child.

slumped
on Beaker's futon,
remembered a three speed
bike, chocolate
birthday cakes, picnics
with potato chips
in dimness my thoughts ran, candle wax

slipped down the sides of an empty
wine bottle, a breeze covered the wick,
the light died

I dreamed
I became
liberty
the liberty bell
cracked

cracked in the heart.
in my skull—yovo give
yovo fuck
yovo take my child
yovo papa hits
yovo yovo you've got
many shoes, what good do you do?
can't carry water, can't wash clothes,
has no baby, gets no man's ding dong,
ding dong the cracked bell rang

I awoke, peed naked under the stars.
Understood freedom and its chains
of loneliness, safer than what many women
called love, accepting repeated slaps,
kicks, orders for apologies, all for a glance
thrown too long at a moon
and its shadows—hiding places
where no one would pummel,
smile, kiss, lie, and pummel
again until fists grew tired
as a baker's

Charles had become very *bien integré* in his village. Sometimes, after listening to his rambles about West African voodoo,
I thought a little too integrated. But the villagers he knew openly
welcomed both of us to many interesting events. The funeral of
a Beninese hero was no exception. A resistance fighter against
the French in the 60's, his funeral had national significance.

Charles invited me, and while I really anticipated seeing a
funeral of this proportion, I mostly just wanted to be with him.
I sensed Charles sliding himself onto a self-designed "higher
plane." I needed him to realize I was as much into Africa as he
was. I started with my appearance. As I tied the waist on my
blue and white *bomba* and asked a Beninese woman to help me
wrap my *foulard,* I thought I looked good. Of course, I had problems finding a bush taxi, and I arrived at the village late. I knew
Charles would already be at the funeral, but how hard could it
be to locate another white person at a funeral?

My bush taxi dropped me off on the side of the road, and for
several minutes I stood and stared at the people standing and
staring at me. In full African costume, I caught them off-guard.
Finally, a local on a moto pulled up, welcomed me to the village
and asked where I wanted to go. I told him I needed to find the
English teacher who was at the funeral. The motoman assured
me it wouldn't be a problem, and after we haggled over the
price, he revved off in the direction of the deceased's first wife's
house. Arriving there, we discovered the body had already been
moved. My driver kept telling people on the street, "See, I got
this white woman who is trying to find the white guy and the
dead guy." Thirty minutes later we found the dead guy at the
church, along with crowds of people.

I told the usher I was late but needed to sit next to the other
yovo. Unfortunately, a group of tourists had caught wind of
the funeral and considered it an attraction. The usher took me
to three different white men before I stopped him and hissed,
"Look at me! Do I look like them? They are wearing T-shirts and
shorts. I want the white person who is dressed as a Beninese."

Renewing his efforts, he made his way through the crowd to the whitey/wanna-be Beninese. Before leaving he asked, "Is he your husband?"

"Yes, we've been married six years and have five children."

Undeterred, he said that if I came to live with him, I could have ten more kids. I blocked that advance by reminding him that I was in a period of mourning; so I couldn't consider his offer.

During the service, stares bounced from me to the Beninese to the tourists and back. I think the villagers were doubtful, yet impressed, that we correctly wore their clothes. The tourists were interested and amused, maybe even contemplating buying some clothes of their own for souvenirs. I just felt plain weird: the Beninese thought I was white; the tourists thought I'd gone native.

Before we could leave for the parties that followed the service, the tourists approached us. They told us facts gleaned from their guide books, suggested fascinating places we needed to see and snapped photos as if the funeral presented itself as a legitimate attraction. After enduring several minutes of stilted conversation, we discovered that we had lost the ability to make small talk and excused ourselves . Reflectively, Charles took my hand and said, "We've changed."

"Yeah."

"It's nice to have you here."

I gave him my biggest smile and did a two-second happy dance before we entered the house of the first party. Pandemonium booty shaking, fast flowing palm wine in abundance, goats and calves roasting on spits next to basins and basins and basins of rice. One man had died, but the entire village was *living*.

I gave Charles a kiss and said that if he died, I would celebrate his presence in the world with an even larger celebration. He squeezed my hand and went to get us some more palm wine.

When woolen socks, a woven rug
and my mother's hug made me smile,

before clubs, drinks, and boys,

when I knew Narnia and was a sprite,
sometimes Tinkerbell, more often Wonder Woman,

I danced, twirling, until dizziness helped me

rediscover dirt. Laughter and glee escaped,
played leap frog across a midnight galaxy
which bored me. I flirted with the baseball team,

outwitted God with philosophy, wined through France,
befriended nicotine, learned Kyle didn't love me,
exiled myself to an African village.

Coconut trees' rigid bark, haughty branches, leaves

shunned me. Weekly doses of malaria medication
did not protect me from hallucinations.
Dreams cajoled me

towards trees that did not speak anymore. Under them,

I scooped sand, swatted away the moonbeams

I no longer inhaled. With the ragged metal
butt of the shovel I found remnants of Tinkerbell's body,

wings sliced off.

AFI
Shadows on the moon—
reassuringly magnificent to me,
but you never regarded them,
had never regarded them,
strained to understand why I did,
then smiled complacently.

Lizards around Beaker's latrine scuttled
over the cardboard cheese box
that was someone's toy,
across the discarded Frisbee
used as a plate.
One day you'll be married

to the pulse of bongo drums
and get beaten
in silence.
You'll bear children
and scar their faces
to ward off evil spirits.

I'll go back to my country
where evil spirits come out
only in stories
I tell while savoring
imported brews on a patio
with others who comment

on your pot of rice,
your calluses,
your latrine
which makes them

remember the plumber
is coming and their Saturn

payments are due
which will remind me
of my next job
interview and the family
luncheon with iced
tea and easy chairs.

During the years my mother created our "austerity program," I slouched. She worried I had low self-esteem. I went to the doctor because of headaches. He, concerned with the slouching, suggested I imagine balloons tied to the nipples of my breasts. I had never heard anyone say the word "breasts." "Nipple" I had heard in reference to sheep udders. Sometimes we milked them. Nipples, as far as I knew, should not be connected to balloons. There was also the whole matter of tying the balloon to the nipple. It would have to be a fairly tight knot. It would have to hurt.

We didn't have money for more doctors' visits. As a role model, I was given our neighbor, Mrs. Alfred Tschetter. Alfred never had to tell Esther to throw her shoulders back. Except when Esther volunteered to drive tractor and got high off the diesel fumes blowing back in her face.

Actually, Esther didn't drive tractor just to get high off the gas fumes,
    that was me.

So much silence. Visits from other volunteers occurred sporadically. Loneliness, loneliness, loneliness. Reading, writing, thinking, missing people, all ways to amuse myself, but none of them made noise: …still just me and the equatorial dust silently swirling around the candle flame.

Weeks passed and I taught English, but the only conversations I had happened in my head, or with my stuffed bat during siesta and right before dozing off into a night of African dreams. My stuffed bat knew everything. Occasionally, I worried my neighbors could hear me talking to no one. They never said anything, probably considering it one more weird characteristic of the *yovo*.

Attempts to make friends with the village women frustrated me, due to my lack of fluency in local languages. With most of them I had no language as shared territory on which to construct a type of friendly understanding. However, even with the women who could communicate with me, I had almost no life experiences over which we could bond.

Besides Big Mama and a few other women, most of them had not gone to school and, therefore, didn't know French. I visited them, but the visits mostly consisted of my sitting on a bench, saying nothing while they sat on a bench saying nothing. Or we would shell peanuts together, or pound peanuts together, but no one talked as the peanut shells piled up, and I coughed when I inhaled fine chunks of the shells. Sometimes my visits reminded me of a bizarre compilation of bad first dates—nobody said much, and I spent the whole time trying to think of ways to politely end the experience.

When a conversation actually did take place in French, it usually led to dramatic increases of knowledge and cultural appreciation on my part. I expanded my hypothesis on common threads in all cultures. Originally, it had included two: beer and sex. Now I added, against the better judgment of the feminist in me, women and shopping. Secretly, I attributed the desire some of the women in my concession had for shopping to the fact that their country had been colonized by the French. I could not accept shopping as an inherent genetic trait.

Between waves of heat rolling off the surrounding tin roofs, we talked about clothes. It was a tradition at Beninese funerals or other large celebrations to have everyone related or close to the person of honor wear clothes made out of the same material. When someone in the village died, a relative would clap at my door, bringing a length of fabric. In that way I knew that I was going to go to an event dressed in the same pattern as everyone else.

For quite some time, the village women had been trying to get me to participate in their savings program. Every week each woman in a group put in ten francs a day and at the end of the week, one woman got all the money to use however she wanted. Then it started the next week with a different woman getting all the money.

This month Big Mama and her friends had started a savings program with one goal in mind: Easter outfits for Christian church. They asked if I had an Easter outfit. I didn't. I told them I wasn't planning on going to church. Big Mama interpreted that as I wasn't going to church because I didn't have clothes for it; so since we were now friends, she signed me up for the savings program, adding she would buy the fabric for me and get the dress made. No hassle for me. I wouldn't have to stop eating mangoes; my Easter dress would just arrive. Then I could go to church with all the village women.

I had never had an Easter dress in the States. What fun. I agreed. There were too many women to argue with and, besides, I liked the fact that they wanted me to hang with them, to do something "girly," like shopping and dressing up. I got excited too. I had a posse. In traditional African outfits, I and *les femmes au village* were gonna strut our stuff. I was back on the social scene.

Weeks passed and I diligently paid ten francs everyday. Once, I tried paying all seventy francs for one week at once.

I wanted to stop worrying about missing the woman when she walked by to collect it. The woman in charge of collecting the money stared at the coins in her palm. Then peered at me, wrinkling her brow. No one paid the whole seventy francs at one time. She explained that I wouldn't be getting the money back until much later. I nodded. Her raw incredulity scared me. I took back sixty francs. I didn't want the village to think I was obscenely rich; so I accepted the ten francs per day rule.

I received the savings program money last. When all had been collected, I quickly handed it over to Big Mama. The women had been talking for weeks about how pretty and feminine the material was. And it was blue. I loved blue. And the idea of wearing something blue and feminine and hanging out with a large group of happy women made me ecstatic. I wanted Easter to arrive, and not because of chocolate bunnies. Life was improving here.

Wednesday before Easter I inspected the new palm leaf fans I had bought at the *marché*. I had started buying gifts to send to people back home. I figured the fans were flat enough to pack and at twenty-five francs, a good deal. Plus, very representative of my time here. I knew my dress should be finished soon. I expected Big Mama to come over at some point and show it to me. I couldn't concentrate on anything more complex than comparing the thickness of the fans' handles, trying to imagine which relative—adult or child—should get each fan. In Africa, I had the time to worry about such things. Often I looked for such things to worry about.

Big Mama arrived with a plastic sack and the woman who had started the whole Easter outfit savings program: Spice Girl. I had no idea if she could sing, but I sensed that if she would have been on a different continent, she would have been part of the group. I got up and quickly got them water. Since Spice Girl appeared, I knew it was important.

Spice Girl said she came along to see how the *bomba* looked on me and, with a pointed look, to make sure I wore it correctly.

I hugged the plastic bag and rushed to my bedroom to change while Big Mama and Spice Girl looked at the snow globe I had on my table. The snow globe had been a gift from a friend in the States. People in my village loved it. So did I. It had snow.

Part of me had been afraid that the dress would turn out ugly. In college my friends, after many late nights of studying at diners and getting service that wasn't always service, invented the saying that realistically, one could expect the hot chocolate, but not the whipped cream. I already knew that for Africa, I had the hot chocolate, and the whipped cream: I had paid for a dress, it had shown up, and on time. I thought I would be stretching my luck if the dress were actually pretty. It was. I held it up in the candle light. Very blue, very feminine, mostly lace. In fact, all lace. I tried it on. Completely see through. It looked like a bizarre outfit to wear in a club in the States. Actually, I wouldn't have worn it, even in the States. Maybe it was a joke?

I took it off and re-entered my living room. Big Mama and Spice Girl put the globe back on the table and stared at me. I asked if the dress was supposed to be all lace. They said yes. I said it was see-through. They said I still had to wear underwear and bra. I said even with underwear and bra, it was see through. You could see my underwear and bra. They said to try it on and show it to them.

I had become closer to Big Mama, but I didn't really want to walk around in front of her in my underwear and bra, draped in a thin layer of blue lace. However, I did. Spice Girl said it looked nice. Big Mama said maybe I shouldn't wear it to church. I didn't. I went to church in one of my frumpf-frumpfs and looked at the group of women wearing blue lace outfits over their dark underwear and dark bras that blended well with their skin so spectators couldn't really see them. On me, you saw lace, skin, underwear. It showcased my "merchandise." Too much. The transparent Easter outfit could have been a cross-cultural misunderstanding, but I suspected not. I suspected Spice Girl, noticing my absent husband, had an agenda.

5

Ten Moons on Fire

R*EVISION*
Goals:
to be a dolphin,
a water angel,
lightning

> *I felt along the concrete floor for my matches,*
> *knocked over my canteen. Noise reverberated,*
> *gelled with croaking frogs.*

the first rain drop,
not the only rain drop

> *My pulse flew like the plane in my dreams. Home*
> *in ten months.*

the moon reflecting a sea on fire

I memorized my mother's letters, ventured into sleep
on the fringes of her memory.
Ten more moons.

Prayer:
Now I lay me down
to tremble
and await the roosters' crows.

During dry season, the part of my house without a roof became my ideal rec room. It didn't have a pool table or dart boards, but it had private space with air movement, was a little cooler than the rest of my house, and the inquiring village eyes could not witness me boogie to the stars and sing for the bats.

Not to mention easy trash disposal. After lunch, I remained lying on my straw mat and just tossed my mango pits over the wall—bonus points if a pit hit one of the local cow herders walking by—double bonus points if it hit one of the local cow herders and then bounced off one of his cows.

I also exercised there. The day I taught my class similes and Ikilou stood with his smile and said, "Madame is as fat as an elephant," spawned an internal debate over whether to rejoice that someone had finally formed a correct simile or to be offended and kick him out. Even though I had lost weight due to my stomach problems, that day served as a catalyst for my African workout plan.

Loneliness also contributed. Brutal loneliness made getting up at five a.m. and biking up hills for two hours in 100° weather to see another American normal.

For my treks, I always left Glazoué at five a.m., but I would undoubtedly still pedal by some of my students who stared and started the *"Yo-vo! Yo-vo! Yo-vo!"* chant as I huffed by in my cloud of sweat.

As the weeks passed, I turned my biking journeys into an adventure movie about AFRICA! *The camera, situated on a sandy path in the quiet, pre-dawn African morning, pans the horizon showing a ribbon of road rising out of the swamp of a village. On that road, bobbing in the distance, a speck. Funky African music starts in the background. The speck increases in size, occasionally disappearing as it goes down a hill only to reemerge larger as it nears the camera. Soon the speck becomes identifiable as a human figure on a bicycle, feet moving up and down. As the figure comes ever closer to the lens, a girl in billowing skirt and sandled feet emerges through the shimmering heat waves radiating from the road since the sun has risen in the time it has taken for her to become life-size. The music swells as the camera goes for the close-up shot. She appears to be pedaling to a specific rhythm, a rhythm which merges with the sounds of "Yovo! Yovo! Yovo! Yovo!" coming from the side of the road as the camera swings left to show locals filtering in from the savanna to form a dark line of chanters. The girl rides on and fades into the distant bright heat, fast becoming once again a speck in the tranquil hills*—but in a movie, the sweat and fatigue wouldn't be included. The girl would never become frustrated with the chanters and just want them to STOP! and she would never come to a realization after an hour and a half of biking up hills in the heat that the people who do the Tour de France must be in incredibly good shape. Most certainly, she would never doubt her ability to actually reach the other village and in the script, she would never ask herself the same questions the people on the side of the road had been yelling since she started, "*Yovo*, what are you doing???? Are you crazy?"

However, my life was not scripted. On the days when getting up early didn't bring a smile to my face or I didn't feel like being village entertainment, I did sit-ups and jumped rope back in the part of my house that didn't have a roof. Even without the roof, the heat was oppressive. The slight breeze didn't prevent the all-over body heat rash worse than my pre-school chicken pox. It propelled me to exercise as "nature girl." I felt liberated exercising naked with the wind on my stomach.

Standing in front of my classes, I felt less frustrated if I had biked on the weekends or gone to my "gym." Students who had seen me on the way out of the village on my bike rides would often come to me after class and tell me they had seen me and yelled *"Yovo."* It created a bond, gave us something to discuss…what exactly was exercise, why did I exercise, how did I decide what kind of exercise to do, how often did I exercise, at what time did I exercise, for how long did I exercise.

One day, after an especially thorough interrogation, I biked to the *marché* and stopped to visit Mama Inez. The path I took home from the *marché* brought me to my house from the back. The fifteen to twenty foot palm trees lining the path were impressive. I stopped, admiring the green of their leaves, splotched with something khaki colored, like student uniforms. The palm trees that overlooked the back of my house that had no roof and so let occasional winds frolic over my bare body as I jumped rope, those palm trees harbored my students—interested in the American concept of exercise.

WRITTEN COMPETENCE IV

Please answer the following questions in short paragraphs. Use complete sentences.

1. In the story, what did Koffi want for his birthday? Why?

2. What types of food did Koffi see in the capital?

3. Do the gendarmes honestly expect me to say, "OK, come inside and let's get it on?"

4. Will the rash on my ass from wiping so much go away when I go back to the States?

5. Why am I too chicken to say anything about the kids getting beaten?

I. BEFORE SIESTA
He strained to lift, balance,
and pour basins or bags of rice and manioc.
His biceps, pecs, and abs—solid,
cut without air-conditioned sweat
in scheduled gym sessions.

During a break, he spun a knifed tire,
mindless of stench, heat, distended
bellies. Unaware he could not model
Gap kids with voodoo scars
on his face.

He saw me stare at the diagonal
slash under the right eye, the horizontal
nick on the forehead. He said, "I will not die
because of Jesus. Thunder roars
and descends on the guilty to cleave their lives
from this world, if the voodoo gods cry
for justice. When thieves ravage goat herds,
the gods breathe fire into the lungs
of a lizard who scampers to exhale,
roasting them alive.

I see you smirk as if I'm drunk.

My people possess secrets
strangers do not understand.
My grandfather commands the Power.
My father listened to you who hung crucifixes
around his neck. No thunder fell when
he pleaded. A fever captured my father;
my grandfather laughed, told him
to pray and didn't come to his funeral."

II. THE JOURNEY
My grandfather came to me and said,
"Come, my little one, come with me
Let's go into the woods
To find The Old One beneath the Talking Tree.

I faced a cloudless sky,
Talked with the wind
And heard from the stars—
They said it's time for you
To know the secrets—
The Old One will die.
But first, my little one, you shall learn.
Within you, the Power shall burn.

We must walk with the sun
Pushing us forward,
Be led by the wind,
And dance through the grass,
Then cross through the stream,
And there—
That's the grey cliff of Okemeré you see
And on top is the Talking Tree.
Its roots grow down, down through the rock
To a hollow place
Where roots and stone meet earth

And man and magic are joined—
Power—swirling from above
And swirling from below.
The Old One inhales the force
And cries to gods for their will—

Today, he'll make gris gris.
Little one, do not fear,
You shall soon understand the wind
And the Spirits are one,

The Old One hums
with them
And pounds
With pestle
In mortar
The roots,
And herbs
And bones
To make dust,
Blessed Dust.
And the people come

To the cliff of Okemeré,
From afar they see the white flag
On the Talking Tree
So they know the Spirits
And The Old One are working.
To The Old One they'll talk—
And he'll look at their faces,
Taking some soul with his glance
To toss in the skin pouch
With Dust and maybe a shell—
The contents depend on the spell.
And that, my little one, is what you shall do—
Listen to the wind and The Old One and learn
To make gris gris for good
And gris gris for bad.

For The Old One is not the God of Falling Thunder
Nor a lizard that breathes fire,
But the gods give him Power,
So from nature he creates
Charms, potions, and powders

To place in a pouch and hang
Around your neck or in your house
To keep Evil away—
Or with different herbs
And a newer bone—
Pounded with a louder chant—
Evil will live
With your neighbor,
Kill all his chickens,
Make his wife barren.

So, go, my little one, go
Your school is there—learn
The secrets that The Old One knows."

Dear Angela,
     How to market Benin to future PCVs: Everyday
is Valentine's Day—candles and meals under the
stars.

P.S. It's not painful to wear clothes today.
My candles actually hold form. The *chaleur* is
over!!

I always tried to mail my packages home during my stays in Cotonou. Small envelopes I trusted to leave Glazoué. However, I feared the mysterious allure of the large padded yellow envelopes heading for my homeland might overwhelm my postman. Older volunteers had confirmed that sometimes arriving packages disappeared a mile or two from their final destinations, and that departing ones often got lost within ten minutes. Their proof of the strange mishaps at the post office came from the random Twizzlers seen in the hands of the postmaster's children. Or the yo-yos that swung through the *marché* stalls controlled by the hands of adults.

To mail a small batik to Angela, I bargained with a *zemijahn* to take me to the new post office. Even though realistically I knew it didn't make any difference, I hoped new might mean faster. I pulled my moto helmet off, paid the *zemijahn* and nearly fell down when the clean, tinted, glass doors slid silently open as I approached. The new post office had doors. Automatic doors. It also had telephones, computers, and faxes. Well-dressed tellers stood behind actual counters. People formed lines. People in Western style suits and heels, carrying leather bags, took checkbooks and credit cards out of wallets and purses. No one haggled or raised a voice. Nothing was wrapped in leaves. I saw only two children, and they wore clothes.

I did not know what to do. This place appeared to have a system. In my purple and white swirly print frumpf-frumpf dress, wearing Tevas, balancing a moto helmet against my hip, and trying to figure out which line I should pick in order to send my re-used duck-taped envelope, I realized I had lived *au village* a long time.

A security guard noticed my frozen state, and probably my dusty feet and pit-stained dress, and offered his assistance. I said I wanted to mail a package. He told me I had come to the right place. I stared at him. Sarcasm? I had forgotten it existed. He laughed, asked me from where I had come.

"Glazoué."

He smiled. "You live there? How do you like it?"

"It's nice." The post office, with its order and expectations that its logic and order would be understood, was causing a meltdown, and I could not think of other things to say.

He pointed to a line, and I took my place behind a man wearing a gold watch and a pendant. He turned to stare. A woman in the next line snapped shut her blush, looked me over, and smirked before turning to start a conversation in French with her boyfriend.

This different, unexpected kind of disrespect stung. I had not experienced the clash between myself and the rich Beninese. These people looked down on me. Like the villagers, they didn't care about my education or life goals either. They didn't care that I had come to work in a village in their country. They didn't understand that impulse or the villages of their country. And I didn't think that any of them would have sent girls over to my house to help me get water or delivered bananas when they knew my friends were over, or laughed and repeated the local word for rice eighteen times until I could say it. The post-office made me homesick, for Glazoué.

I knew the hot taxi ride had made me a little smelly, and I hadn't shaved in months, but when the woman and her make-up compact slid away from me, clinging to her boyfriend, I wanted to tell them I wasn't contagious, that poverty wasn't contagious, just hard, and for their country, dangerous.

MIDTERMS—

Write your autobiography (name, age, family, education, goals)

1. I call myself Rachidi.

2. I am one brother two sisters.

3. I go to Sorbonne CEG Glazoué.

4. The member of my mother are two sisters and one
brother.

5. After school, I want to do a doctor.

Beauty: a gravity-trailer full of heavy, dry corn during a
good year. There are women who know this and who know they
are worth something when their men are well fed at 10:00 and
noon and 4:00 and 6:30. Women who understand they won't
take a vacation because sheep prices fell and the bank needs a
payment for the cultivator.

They love men who nurture tractors, handle baling twine,
and understand the breeding phases of the moon. Their daughters understand the eyes of the boys on the shearing crew.

Even in sixth grade with skinny chicken legs and no breasts,
I felt the eyes of the boys and the men when I brought the trays
with food out to them during their breaks from shearing. My
sister must have also. When shopping, she chose a swimsuit
with ruffles on top so no one could tell her breasts were bub-
bling. No one told her that breasts made her a woman. And that
was good.

She wore her blond hair short. Her closet had men's flannels
that were two sizes too big for her. She was strong.

When the tractors broke, Dad sent us into town to get a
new part: two fidgeting blond girls standing five feet from the
counter at the implement dealer, trying to remember the type
of spark plug our dad needed. Often, the guys at the implement
dealer gave us the wrong part.

The men working the scale at the elevator might not weigh
gravity boxes of grain accurately, the mechanic might charge
twice for labor, and the vet might arrive late so the ewe with
the prolapse would die, but they came from German Farmers:
Men of the Church and Land. In the pastures, male animals

humped and bucked and got fed extra oats for their numerous conquests.

Elsewhere, women had gone through a decade of indignity. They organized protests and gave speeches. Women who were not virgins got married or chose not to. They wrote dissertations and became separate, educated entities, creating their own definitions.

No one in my hometown had burned a bra. The crackle of flames made noise.

I wanted to be strong enough to handle Africa alone, enough of a woman not to need a man, but I knew my secret desire to love. To my friends I denied that I wrote Charles poems and mailed them to him. Then I wrote him more poems in my journal and didn't send them to him but read them over and over at night. The wind would blow my candle out, and I would search for more matches.

If I look at yesterday afternoon as an example, I could say Charles did not possess me. Yesterday in 104° weather with palm trees, sand paths, and latrines, I remembered Julie, a classmate in elementary and high school. I hadn't talked to her since the Memorial Day band concert in the city cemetery the Monday after our high school graduation. Although through the small town Midwestern gossip chain that my mother participated in, I had heard she lived in Utah.

I wondered if Julie knew I was in Africa. I wondered that about everyone. I wanted to know if people back home thought about me. Every morning my friends, family, relatives, and people in my hometown must have gotten up with some concern for me. Did they think, "Monique is in the deep dark continent of Africa. *National Geographic* does specials on that place. It's scary there." I felt better thinking that people thought of me. I always imagined Charles thought of me, and for the villagers and other PCVs we continued to pretend to be in love until I forgot it was pretense.

On my bike ride home, I stopped by Mama Inez's stand to

get food for the evening. A hard afternoon rain had packed the sand. Biking did not cause me as much consternation as usual. I could turn corners without the fear of my wheels slipping and my dress getting tangled in the chain as I tried to stop myself from falling. Understandably, the villagers found my falls entertaining. Coming from the States, I misread their amusement at my clumsiness as malicious. Big Mama finally told me after several months it was often no more than surprised bewilderment that I, supposedly educated, could not perform basic tasks.

Many of my *quatriéme* students gathered in the road in front of me as I neared the intersection of the paths leading to my house and to Mama Rita's house. They watched me bike up in my frumpy dress and dirty Tevas to the newly formed puddle. I didn't dismount. I stopped, straddling the bike with my dress draped on the boy's bar and regarded the water covering the path. It didn't look too deep, but I asked for confirmation. My students smiled at me with my backpack full of rice, fried yams, and pineapples. "Yes, Madame, yes, you can bike through this. It is not deep."

On my toes I pushed backwards several feet in order to build momentum when I hit the puddle. Even though most villagers wondered how I managed to live—I had no calluses on my hands, no scars on my arms, no cooking or water-carrying skills, no defined muscles,—I did have the common sense to anticipate mud, regardless of how shallow the puddle was.

Technically, it wasn't a puddle. A stream ran on either side of the path but, normally, people using the path could walk through without a problem since the path had been built up slightly higher than the stream. During the sprinkles the previous week, before the rainy season had really started—although I did not know that—I thought the sprinkles were the rainy season—the villagers simply put in large rocks. They then hopped across from stone to stone. The stones had convinced me to take the path mindless of the afternoon rain. Previously I had, not gracefully, but still successfully, maneuvered my bike across the rocks. The villagers had certain paths for the rainy season. Others they avoided.

My students had watched me bike towards the large puddle. They ran ahead, yelled in Fon, and gathered their classmates to witness me and my famous bike cross the puddle.

Again I questioned, "Are you sure?"

"Yes, Madame, yes," they said, "we are sure."

With one hand I pulled my skirt up on both sides to reduce the splash effect. I put my right foot and all my weight on my pedal and took off. The puddle engulfed me. The water leveled off at my waist. I couldn't pedal. I couldn't balance. It wasn't bikable. I fell into the water and the sensation of being wet, completely drenched, instantly brought back the information I learned in my three months of in-country medical training about schisto, leeches, giardia, and snakes.

"Fuck....fuck! Fuck Africa. Fuck you."

Some children shouted above their laughter, "Madame, Madame it is not safe in the water. Get out. Get out. It is not good in the water."

"Fuck you. Mother fucking A."

I righted my bike and sloshed my way out of the puddle. The children scampered away. Most of them did, the smart ones did. Ikilou stayed and started to walk home with me.

"Madame, are you OK? To be in the water is not good."

"I know, Ikilou. I didn't know the water was so deep."

"Well, it is rainy season now. Not all roads are good. You want me to help you clean your bike?"

"No."

"Madame, when you were in the water, what were you yelling in English?"

"'Fuck you,' Ikilou. I said 'fuck you.' "

"That means 'help me?' "

"Yes."

To help Ikilou commit the phrase to memory we chanted "'fuck you" all the way to my house. Julie crossed my mind. In the fourth grade I had invited her over to the farm after school. We didn't have cable, Atari, Barbies, or fashion magazines. I got my sister's blue three-speed bike out of the chicken shed, and Julie and I took turns riding it around the driveway. The day before, my dad had pumped the sewer. Our farm didn't have a connection to any sewer line. When we moved there, my dad bought a big pump. He emptied the cesspool every couple of weeks. Since we had no place to put it, the drainage flowed into the ditch alongside the driveway. I don't remember, but it must have reeked.

Julie and I both loved Gonzo from the Muppets. Julie thought water, not very deep water, filled our ditch. I dared her to pretend to be the Great Gonzo and ride my sister's bike through it. She did. She fell off in the middle. Neither my mother nor Julie found the incident amusing. My mom took her home immediately. In the village, I knew no one was going to take me home; so I got out my antiseptic body scrub and started to eradicate all the prancing microbes in my pores.

I scrubbed until I felt cleaner, but not less angry and humiliated. Several times every week, usually more than once a day, I did something that made the villagers chuckle. I told myself they laughed with me, not at me. I didn't believe it. None of the cross-cultural training that PC gave me my first three months had prepared me for being an incompetent idiot in the village. The villagers would now add trying to bike through a puddle/swamp to the large list of incompetencies I had already established: couldn't bargain at the *marché,* couldn't carry water on my head, couldn't sweep with a palm leaf broom, didn't have a permanent man in the house. In their eyes, the first three caused the last one. Big Mama never hesitated to point out Charles did not visit often.

SATURDAY AFTERNOON AT BEAKER'S
still
air, hot
body, spiked
hair, tumbling mind,
empty stomach, blistered

hands of Afi.
Together we would dance,
her khakis sweaty
in the sun, me not thinking
of empty mailboxes.
A drumming of love.
She and I felt sun,
sweat,
soul.

And then mine reared:

Don't settle.
Please.
Don't need.
Show me wild. Show me dirty.
Show me you can surpass the wind,
Or at least shimmy up a tree,
Scuff your shins and smile and bleed.
Show me.
Show me.

Remember where you're from
there are no bush taxis or sacrifices or 120^0 afternoons
spent in unair-conditioned tin structures.

Remember where you're from
there are escalators, ice cube machines, and stores with
roofs.

Where you're from you don't light your house with
candles bought from a woven basket on top of a
woman's head. And rats don't run through bars while
paraplegic polio victims beg for francs.
Where you're from there are televisions and radios that
don't talk about
where you're at.

Afi returned with mangoes
and my soul quieted.
For now, this is where I'm from.

Dear Angela,
    If you want to know what kind of day I've
had, smell me.

AFRICAN WINTER
If I drowned in my own sweat,
would it be a catastrophe,
mosquitoes' wings quivering
into silence?
Loneliness means at one time I had
friends.

I watched a praying mantis give birth
on my lantern. A non-magical lizard
knocked over my water bottles.

Butt calluses mean at least I have a chair.

Through the holes in the roof,
bats swished. Another praying mantis
landed on my back. With my hand,
I killed it.

Anger means before there was calm.

I wanted to slip into my bed, a moist dungeon.
Sand dunes replaced snowdrifts
creating low visibility due to dust particles,
not snowflakes, but no one cancelled school.

I cursed Papa Afi to the polar bears
on my calendar—icy, furry, and freezing.

When the sun went away but forgot
its heat in my bedroom, I sat
on my straw mat, meditating

on ice cream, fans, igloos, snow cones,
popsicles, hypothermia, wind chills,
Dairy Queen, snowmen, making snow
angels naked—numbing every cell.

In the morning I brushed my hair,
smiled at a lizard
instead of you.
Against a concrete wall
I leaned my head.
Where was your chest?

Dear Angela,
    A slow day. I read the back of one of the
anti-bacterial hand-washes I packed in the
States. The instructions say it kills 99.9% of
all common germs. The worrisome word: common.

In jr. high I learned
to sing

"shut de door keep out de devil
shut de door keep de devil
in de night
shut de door keep out de devil
light a candle everytins alright
light a candle everytins alright"[3]

for many years, I sang
it didn't work

When I was smaller, younger, a child, a person-others-
considered-a-child, not yet an adult, I knew the stars needed
me, knew that I needed them. I plastered myself outside on our

gravel driveway. Never on the grass, never on top of one of the round bales, it had to be the gravel. In my ski jacket, mittens, scarf, boots, and ski cap I pressed pressed pressed into the cold hard gravel, grounding myself as I gazed. I needed to take the stars in. To float as they did. To be majestic. To be away. In college I took astronomy, my chance to look through the observatory telescope and truly see the stars. But it was physics. Astronomy was physics. It ruined the stars for me. There was only one night of observation. After two weeks, I dropped the class.

I fell for my first super-intellect, Kyle. He thought I was nice, fun to tease, someone to debate, someone to corrupt. He insisted stars were math. Equations. He put logic next to a nebula. He got rid of the mystery. He rationalized the stars, publicly admitted all he saw in life was logic. He felt safe with the known.

I argued we were stars too. That the wind had smacked some dust on us and the dust came from the stars, a gift, creating a connection between all humanity. Therefore, we had a responsibility to respect and nurture one another. When I mentioned the whispers at night, the tugs, the twists on the insides, the inklings, the intuition, when I said I had those, and he did too and that they all came from the stars, the stars that he wanted to categorize and name as if he were God, he scoffed and poured me a shot of whiskey and then took me to the bars to watch humanity connect.

I learned looking for the wind made me "weird," talking to the stars lowered my I.Q. For him, I tried logic. I bowed to his intelligence and strength. I put chunks of my soul in my jacket pockets, humility in storage boxes at home, mutual respect in the top drawer of my desk, and under the mattress of my bunk bed I shoved the idea of consideration. Then the stars couldn't find me. They saw my body walking around, but did not recognize it. My stardust lay shelved behind Kyle's Bacardi Limon. The wind whipped around me. It cried. I put on my headphones and walked through it. When it still bothered me, I went inside to find blankets and Monday night football with Kyle. And cigarettes.

I forgot about the wind and how when sirens wailed I used to pray to angels. When I looked in my closet, I searched for the heels to match the lavender blouse for Kyle's house parties. I did not try to find the weak spot in the back of the closet wall. I had come to understand Narnia didn't exist.

Kyle got bored with teasing, frustrated with my semi-present resistance. I tired of drinking. With my applications for graduate school and TV jobs, I also included my application for the Peace Corps. When I received notification from Peace Corps that they had accepted me for service in Africa, I remembered. I remembered I had been taught people should take responsibility for humanity. I remembered I used to believe trees had kissed the stars to birth me. Branches had grabbed chunks of stardust to flatten out to make my skin. The wind had carried it down to them. It had heard me calling to it from the darkness. The stars knew they wanted me to have part of them, that the earth needed me with star dust to prance around, to expose my bare neck to the moon, to speak French and Tree. I thought it was time to find my vertebrae.

Kyle smirked, then laughed aloud and found other women for his drinking and philosophy sessions. Weeks later at eleven on a Saturday night, he called. Most of his friends had left for the bars, but he had missed my divine presence at his New Year's party. He and his best friend, nicknamed the preening weasel, had been debating star power, and they needed an expert opinion. Part of me missed Kyle and the challenge of his sly smirk. I bundled up and drove over to have a drink and start their new year with enlightenment.

I drove back to the dorm late the next morning remembering:

"shut de door keep out de devil
shut de door keep de devil in the night
shut de door keep out de devil
light a candle everytins alright
light a candle everytins alright"[3]

it hadn't worked,
the preening weasel came
in me, the devil came
in me, he came forced,
my first time, and so I did
not sing, I went
to the cornfields
I went to the corn
fields of corn, harvested,
no corn just stalks,
stiff stalks, brittle, used
for prayer I whispered

"amazing grace how
sweet the sound that
saved a wretch
like me"

wretch witch
bitch beer bitch
bring him some beer
bitch, I was
the beer bitch

brought him some
beer and then
then he raped
raped raped raped me
I brought him beer
and then he gave
he gave me reason
to grasp stalks
to gasp to stalks
a reason to stalk
my soul, it was
dead, behind closed doors
he came and I didn't
talk, couldn't talk.....

And now, I was surprised, happy, and worried that my heart still warmed and quickened around Charles, another super-intellect.

He told me, in a moment meant to be poetic,
that the wind, like a person,
was only noticed when it touched something.

Sometimes, I thought it could take me away.
Usually, I thought it was the voice of God.

We were in a shelter from the barren landscape,
no evidence of wind.

The first time I was surrounded
by sand and wind and this man,
I thought it was love.

*He softened his lips with chapstick
to ease the burn and tilted his face
downward to avoid the sun and the wind.
Should I kiss his faded freckles
and unchafed lips, lips that didn't turn
to the god voice and try to swallow it,
to surround it, to be it.*

*Last week, I thought the wind was angry
with me. I slept with my windows
open and it blew rain in, but only
at night. Why didn't the wind
want me to sleep? Why didn't God
want me to rest? I doubted this man could
tell me. I didn't ask.*

*He loosened a lace, pretended to philosophize.
Where had he tucked his laughter?
It was not good to tuck laughter
anywhere, to say "fuck laughter."
It was almost a sin.*

6

Nine Moon Shadows

HOT ENOUGH FOR SPONTANEOUS COMBUSTION, I MOVED slower than a slug, tranquilized.

On the side of the path next to a *marché* mama and bananas, a plate of popcorn.

Love at first sight suddenly became clear.

My pale hand pillaged the plate, stuffing the foreign treasure in my *marché* bag. I coaxed my melting body back to my house, closed my eyes, pretended the warm beer was chilled, and with the first munch of a kernel transported myself back to the theater on 41st and Western—remembering the red cushions, the sticky floor, listening to the details of Angela's last date. The music swelled, scenes from someone else's imagination occupied the screen and my mind.

The popcorn tumbled down my throat. An empty bag. I opened my eyes, asked a fly why my life did not have a soundtrack. As I squatted on my concrete block to scrub my white cotton underwear, I stopped occasionally to listen for the swell of the "everything works out" theme for this African scene.

Not all the volunteers taught English. Some of them started rural community development projects. Often I bemoaned the fact that English was not really what the people needed. I felt I could do more if I started rural community development projects. Savings plans, infant nutrition, birth control, wood conservation, people needed/wanted that type of information. I could present them skills they could use right away, and then I would see results before my two years were up. Paul, a volunteer who had almost finished his two years of service, had the job of going out into remote villages, (by African standards, Glazoué was not remote) and giving seminars on accounting and budgeting.

Each seminar lasted several hours, usually due to the amount of translating involved. He didn't speak the local languages, or much French; so before each seminar he painstakingly looked up every word for his speech. The task consumed hours of his time but, for some reason, never helped him improve his French. Instead, he found French-speaking counterparts from his village who also spoke the local languages of the people he was planning to educate. He packed an English/French dictionary in his backpack and they tromped through the savannah to talk about numbers.

The villagers assembled. Paul explained budgets in French; the counterpart translated. Paul pointed to the posters he had made—in French. The translator also pointed to the numbers and charts and disseminated the information in the local language. The process to explain the process of keeping a monthly budget took hours. If Paul's escapades crossing the savannah—which often included getting lost, ripping a shoe, and taking diarrhea breaks—made him reach the village in the late morning, the session would not get started before lunch. He spent the morning holding his poster, sitting on a bench drinking some *tchouk*, if he were lucky. Or, if not lucky, just sitting on a bench, watching flies use his poster as a latrine.

On those days, he would start sharing his knowledge in the

late afternoons. At the end of the day, before rolling up his now smeared brown poster with columns and rows of digits, Paul would ask if there were any questions. In Okemeré, one of the villagers said, "Yes, why aren't the flies biting you?" Paul said he was wearing insect repellent. The man asked if Paul could come back next week with some more insect repellent, and then they could talk about budgeting.

Dear Angela,
    Oh, the weather outside is frightful, the
goat head was quite delightful, my green bike
is ready to go, let it snow, let it snow, let it
snow.

I took a taxi forty kilometers to Dassa, the nearest phone, to call the Peace Corps doctor to tell him about my infection. That was three days ago, when I could still open my mouth. He said he would stop by when the next Peace Corps car went north.

I haven't been to school. My cheek is swollen to the point I can't talk. Out of "concern," most of my students stopped by to see Madame and the *choses-la*. I can't greet them. I shuffle my puffy self to the door and look at them. They stare and mumble something about curses from God for women who don't have husbands.

Today the big, shiny, air-conditioned Moving Heaven (SUV) cruised up to my house. The doctor surfed a waft of cool air as he hopped out to look at my cheek. "Yes, you do really have an infection. Did you cut yourself shaving?"

I squinched my eyes and shook my head "no." He repeated the question in English as if I hadn't understood his French the first time, "Did you cut yourself shaving?" I raised my eyebrows and to keep throbbing to a minimum slowly shook my head again, "no." He insisted, "If you cut yourself shaving and didn't disinfect it, even a small cut, it could have gotten infected with staph."

I didn't want to call him Doctor Dufus. I would have liked to call him just Doctor and be thankful when he gave me medical advice, but, couldn't he see that I had never shaved my face? Most women, even Beninese women, didn't shave their faces.

Before he told his chauffeur to turn the radio back up and roared off in the climate controlled, US taxpayer owned SUV, leaving me alone in the sunset, he pulled out an unmarked bottle of pills and told me to take eight of them a day for two weeks and my face would deflate.

If I have kids, I hope they won't come out with three legs.

BEAKER WARNED ME
Weeks passed,
flowers and grass died,
unlike my memories of you.

I tried to write it all down,
loosening the images socketed
in the crook of my soul.
But still I sat on that bench,
sucking mango pits,
thinking of you.

There was no language
for how I felt when you touched
me, nor for how I felt
when you didn't.

There were moans
originating from a place
I didn't know before you.
Some were squelched
in a beautiful ripping,
the others didn't stop.

My dream, a crushed tarantula
on my inner thigh, awoke me.
It had been someone's
wedding day.

I am a poet. I wrote you
a love letter. You didn't write back.

In second grade, I ran away.
I did not know grown-ups

still did.

Friendships get tested in many ways. Jealousy over boy-friends, squabbles over the borrowed shirt that got stained, the nick on the car, the bad birthday present. I had friendships end because of those factors. As I put more antibiotic salve on my index and middle finger and then tenderly, with my eyes almost squinted shut, separated Beaker's butt cheeks so I could rub the salve on the bleeding sores, I thought to myself that I had never tested a friendship in this manner.

Five minutes earlier, she had done the same for me. I had been crying when we finally reached Agadez after several days in the Sahara on camels. There were four of us, only three good camel saddles. How bad could a bad camel saddle be? I didn't think it would inflict bodily injury; so I took it.

In our turbans, without shoes, and bags and bags of oral re-hydration solution, and a guide, we set off into the swirling sand. Astride an arrhythmic animal having no concept of WHOA, I wanted another soundtrack to blur my fear of a giardiasis attack because I had no idea how to stop and dismount this desert machine and no idea where to squat privately in this stark and empty place.

Three hours later we halted. Nothingness, only the soft hint of the L'Air Mountains broke the horizon line far in the distance. A solitary noise, the wind, lifting particles of sand into the yellow sky. Then the swooshiswish of movement, as our guide walked ahead to fill canteens from a well—no sign, no marker—just suddenly a well in the middle of Nothingness. I admired this guide. I idolized this guide. I did not want to lose this guide and die in the desert.

The water he poured into my Nalgene could have passed as a liquefied Dairy Queen blizzard, yellowish with brownish chunks. I added kool-aid, iodine and oral re-hydration salts. In the desert, any drink is a good drink. Leaving the well, I sank into the muffled sound of hooves on sand and accepted the discordant jolting from my long-legged companion. My butt hurt, but the first complaint would not come from me.

At noon a small cluster of thin and wrinkly trees materialized and we stopped. As the camel tilted forward to a kneeling position, I desperately braced my bare feet against his neck. Once my toenails sank into the sand, I tentatively stretched, then patted my butt. It hurt. It stung with even my most gentle of steps. The other volunteers laughed and ripped open bags of dates as we waited for our guide to cook up spaghetti. They plopped down in shady places in the sand and practiced wrapping their turbans in new styles. I stood.

"How can you sit? Don't your butts hurt?"

"No. Why?"

"Mine feels raw. Scraped raw."

"Maybe you should adjust the way you sit. Or don't run your camel."

I had challenged our guide to a race—a two minute race. After those two minutes my leg muscles quivered from the strain of maintaining my balance on this rolling-jolt of a critter, and I accepted defeat. No one mentioned that the guide had said my camel had a bad saddle.

Standing, I snarfed up the spaghetti. Then inching over to my camel, which the guide patiently held by inserting his two fingers into the animal's nose, I clamored aboard in slow motion. Piles of sand cavorted with one another; the wind teased particles into the air and over the hooves of our camels; sweat puddled on my stomach. Solitude. Escape. Relaxation. Only in a travel brochure. My taut thigh muscles pleaded for release from the strain of keeping me balanced. No energy for me to gaze wistfully at sand dunes. And my butt. Something was dreadfully wrong. The sweat that ran down my crack...stung, stung, stung, an acid sting.

That evening, we drank Tuareg tea and spread blankets on the hard sand, direct starlight on our faces all night. We sang and talked of smores. I rolled off my blanket, found my flashlight, some toilet paper, and walked a bit from the group. I needed to scope out my pain. I squatted, pulled my cheeks apart, and patted. Still squatting, I shined the flashlight on the paper. Blood. Bad camel saddle. I let myself cry. On most PCV group trips, there was one person who ruined the adventure for the rest. I didn't want to be that person, but I couldn't get back on that camel.

Everyone drank two cups of Tuareg tea at breakfast and quickly wrapped their turbans in the traditional style before heading over to the camels. I said my butt was really sore from the bad camel saddle. No one said anything. I said I thought the bad camel saddle should be shared. No response. I said we all paid the same to come on the trip, and we should take turns with the saddles. Silence. Beaker stepped up and said she would take it today, and then someone else could take it tomorrow.

I stuck toilet paper in between my butt cheeks and mounted my camel. This saddle was better, but not total comfort. When we dismounted for the night, Beaker was in tears.

The third day. The bad saddle. No one wanted it. Beaker and I walked tenderly around the camp filling our Nalgene bottles, conscious of our leg movements. Our guide saddled up the camels. One of the other volunteers said she had gotten dysentery during the night and couldn't take the bad saddle. The other one said there was no sense in all of us suffering. Beaker and I already were hurt. We might as well finish off the trip by sharing the camel. We looked at her as she quickly walked over to her camel and crawled onto her good saddle. The victim of dysentery did the same. I sighed. Beaker glared. The guide said we had to get moving. Beaker volunteered to take the first part of the day.

That night we returned to Agadez. Tears dropped as I dismounted my camel. Some god-awful unknown African infection would settle in my wound, festering and rotting until I could not walk, all because when I went to Africa and tried to save the world I spent my money on a camel caravan vacation instead of helping to pay for Ikilou's new English books.

Asking Beaker, the specialist on tropical infectious diseases, if we could really get anything in our butts, since it was such an isolated area, was a bad judgment call on my part. I dug out my antibiotic cream and went to the latrine to smear some on my sores, but I could not tell if I smeared it where it needed smearing. Back in her hostel room, Beaker was having the same problem. We promised not to really look, and not to tell anyone that we had smeared salve on each other's butt cracks.

    Tips for camel caravans
        1. Wear pants
        2. Buy turban
        3. Do not wear shoes

4. Make sure camel is sitting
5. Place wooden saddle on camel.
6. If camel stands up, have someone insert fingers into camel's nostrils
7. Move to left side of camel
8. Make sure camel is sitting
9. Make huge effort to swing leg onto neck of camel
10. Do not flinch when camel bellows
11. Put feet on either side of camel's neck
12. Do not jump off when camel bellows
13. Brace self as camel stands
14. Do not be frightened
15. Control speed and direction with feet
16. Bounce against wooden saddle to "unrhythm" of camel gallop
17. Ignore screaming thigh muscles
18. Do not get blisters in butt crack

Dear Angela,
Last night I finished *The Book of Laughter and Forgetting*. It states, "A woman who has remained true to her inner self takes pleasure in everything: eating, drinking, urinating, defecating, touching, hearing, or just plain being."
In 30 seconds, I remembered numerous times here when eating, drinking, urinating, and defecating have been less than pleasurable.

I made a feeble attempt to squelch the *marché* mamas' gossip about my inabilities. Big Mama's rooster cut short my five hours of sweaty sleep and dreams about Dairy Queen blizzards.

I started my morning rant. *How dare the villagers laugh at me? I graduated with honors from college. I moved to a different continent all by myself. I know how to use a computer. They don't even understand the concept of a computer. I have read more books than there are in the whole village. I am a competent woman.*

I rolled out from under the mosquito net and went to the back of my house to find the Nigerian plastic basin. I grudgingly put on one of my frumpf-frumpf dresses, gave myself a pep talk, and left the house.

I walked the half-mile to the water source without meeting anyone. The kids were all in school, the men in the fields, and the women still cleaning up from feeding everyone in the morning. I filled my basin of water three-fourths full. Even with determination I would never be able to balance a full basin of water on my head. I squatted, lifted the basin to my head and slowly, while holding my breath, stood up. The water stayed in the basin which stayed on my head. The surprise made me take a sudden step back, almost spilling the water, but I steadied the basin with one hand and started the slow shuffle back to my house.

I'd like to hear Akala say that I'll never get a husband because I lack skills. I can't wait for Pelagie to come by my house later in the afternoon and ask me if I need her to get me water because the answer will be—"No, actually Pelagie, I don't need you to get me water. I got my own today." And then she'd say, "Oh, you already sent Fulberte to get your water?" I'd say, "No, I got it myself. I carried it on my own head all the way to my house. Then I dumped it into my clay jar all by myself. So, run along and play your clapping games with Fulberte."

Then Pelagie, thinking I would be lying, would run over to Big Mama and ask if I really had carried my own water in a basin on my head. I planned to strut right in front of Big Mama shelling peanuts under the mango tree. She would have to verify my triumphant entry into womanhood.

The moment of finally mastering one skill that qualified me

to be a woman invigorated me. The village could no longer classify me a mere *yovo* who couldn't bike in the sand or eat with her hands without making a mess. I was WOMAN!!

I neared my house and started to sing Whitney Houston's *Queen of the Night*—*I got the stuff that you want, I got the thing that you need*. I strode powerfully, womanly, in front of Big Mama and tripped on an invisible pebble. The basin slipped, doused me with its contents. Big Mama chortled. Then laughed. I picked up my basin, left my dignity, and stomped into my house, re-emerging with my bike.

"*Yovo*, what are you doing? You can't carry water walking; you sure aren't going to be able to carry it while you're on your bike."

"I'm not going to get more water."

"*Yovo*, you want me to send Pelagie to get you water?"

"No, I don't need water."

I had suddenly decided to be the first human who could survive without water.

For an hour, I biked in the direction of the capital until exhaustion and months without potassium cramped my calves. I rested in the dirt. I had been abrupt in leaving Big Mama. My departure would only reinforce her idea of me as an incomplete woman. I wanted her to like me. I needed her to send Pelagie to my house to help me get water—the ride made me reverse my earlier decision—I needed to apologize.

Biking back to my house, I passed a woman selling bush rat. Big Mama loved bush rat. The perfect appeasement—giving a gift would save face without actually apologizing. I slowed my bike to ask the *vendeuse* how much she wanted for a rat.

She did not even glance at me. "*Yovo*, these are rats."

"I know, how much do you want?"

"These are *agouti*.....rats.... *yovos* don't eat rats."

I hadn't convinced myself that I wanted to buy a dead rat, strap it on the back of my bike, and then actually touch it while presenting it to Big Mama. The *vendeuse's* insinuation that I shouldn't have the rat because of my *yovo* status taunted me.

"I understand that they are rats. How much?"

I took out 1000 francs.

She laughed and shook her head.

I took out 1500 francs.

She shook her head again.

2000.

Again the head shake.

2500.

"No."

Taking a taxi from my village to the capital cost 2,500 francs. A rat could not cost more. I cussed and started to pedal away.

'*Yovo!* Come back. Which do you want?'

I picked out a fat male rat, tied him on the back of my bike, and continued home, content.

Being the second wife, Big Mama never got gifts. I untied the rat and presented it to her. She screamed. Neighbors suckling babies and kids on their way home from school searched out the commotion.

My rat impressed people. Seeing my bike with me, they asked where I had gone to buy it. Jokingly, I told them I had biked into the bush and killed it.

Mama Rita scoffed. "*Yovo* didn't kill that rat."

Big Mama stepped forward, "Mama Rita, if *Yovo* said she killed the rat, she killed the rat. Are you saying a friend of mine is lying? *Yovo* killed this rat, right?"

Stunned by Big Mama's usage of the word "friend" in relation to me, I cancelled all intentions of explaining the sarcasm in my statement. "Yes, I killed that rat."

"*Yovo*, no one here believes that you caught that rat. You can't buy rice. Tell us how *you* went on a rat hunt."

I'd been in the village for months. I had eaten rat several times before without any idea how the villagers actually caught them. I never asked them about rats because I feared they would

think the question a hint about wanting one and then go get me
one. And I never had an urge for rat.

"Ummmm, you want to know how I killed the rat?"

"Yes."

"Well, first......."

Big Mama looked at me. "First, she got a stick."

"Ummm, yeah, first I got a stick," I said.

"and then she went into the bush." Big Mama crouched to
show how I went into the bush.

"Yes, and then I went into the bush," I said and crouched
also.

"She saw the rat and she chased after it."

"Right, I saw the rat hidden in the bush and when it ran, I
chased after it."

"When she caught the rat, she beat it like this." Big Mama's
strong arms poised themselves over the dead rat, pretending to
beat it.

"Yes, I beat it dead with my stick," I said, vigorously demon-
strating how I beat the rat.

The crowd of people gathered around Big Mama clapped,
satisfied with the story of "the hunt." Mama Rita went back to
her baby. The school kids trudged back to the dirt path towards
home. I wheeled my bike towards my door. Big Mama wasn't
looking at me, but she had used the word *friend*. I went inside
and waited for Pelagie to come home so I could ask her to help
me get water.

In the part of my house with no roof
lantern shadows caressed concrete
walls, and the moon
shone and the stars
shone and I sang.

I sang
until I forgot the heat,
my hibernating heart.
I sang
thinking about pitch, tone
and reverberations.
I sang to frogs and bats
and with crickets.
I sang
until my voice bonded with the clouds
which carried it away
so it could rain

down on those I loved.
The wick burned out,
still I sang,
eyes shut,
with the moon on my cheeks,
closer to levitation than reality.
I sang
until I didn't sing.
There just was song—
from veins and capillaries,
cracks in my toenails
and pores in my back—

resounding across the swamp.
The song,
my song
had awakened
and I felt again the stars,
saw the moon that had been eclipsed.

DEAR FRIENDS,
I am
the daughter of a crocodile
bred with a lion. I live
full-throttle.

In 110⁰, I bike miles
every day to find rice.
In front of an empty mailbox,
there are no tears, only triumphant
beads of sweat raining into the sand.

I talk to my Puffalump, which I shoved
in my bag only after my mother's prodding,
to practice my French.

And exhaustion, not love,
made me curl up
next to Charles when he visited,
so when he said he didn't care
if someone else kissed me,
I laughed—
until he left the village.
Then on my straw mat,
with sweaty legs curled up to my chin,
I wept.

His presence was my attempt at beauty.

Monique Maria Schmidt

JFK'S 1961 INAUGURAL ADDRESS
IN REFERENCE TO PEACE CORPS
"TO THOSE PEOPLES IN THE HUTS AND VILLAGES OF HALF THE GLOBE
STRUGGLING TO BREAK THE BONDS OF MASS MISERY, WE PLEDGE OUR BEST
EFFORTS TO HELP THEM HELP THEMSELVES, ..."

FOR CHARLES, ONE DAY AFTER DOGON
I knew I loved you
when I agreed to go trekking
with you through the Sahara
to see the Dogon villages.

When I lacerated my toe crawling
down the crevice in the cliffs
outside of Djigibombo,
your brown eyes kept me
following you.

On our second day,
when I got amoebic dysentery
I didn't want your smile
to get too far ahead of me.
I scooped holes in the sand
and squatted quickly.

When our guide crossed paths
with his nomadic drinking buddies
and eventually left
with them, leaving us
with dry Nalgene bottles,
you reinforced your strength
with my re-hydration salts.

158

Your wisdom started us walking
to the west where a village might have been—
sand, sun, sand, sun, sand
no village, no water,
sun, sand, sun, sand, sun.
My toe, my amoebas, my soul
could trudge no further.
The Sahara had won.
I crumpled into the sand,

but you marveled at our luck—
our crusade had led us
past an ancient, solitary altar,
built with three straight rows
of polished skulls.
You speculated about tribal ownership,

I wondered—
when they cut a person's heart out,
as his eyes follow the hand that pulls
away from his chest and air sticks in his throat,
for how many seconds would his brain register
that the beating organ belongs to him—
one, two, maybe three?

When his eyes look at the heart
pulsing in open air
would he ponder who would inherit his Porsche,
remember kisses under the baobab tree,
thirst for the Foster's he bought, but would never drink,
muse over who's invited to the cannibal feast?

If they ever cut your heart out, dear,
don't worry,
I'd be there—

hungry for dinner.

```
Dear Angela,
   I am tired of being vulnerable, of worrying
about the villagers,
of sharing myself with others.
   I want to be young and stupid and frivolous.
My limits stun me.
```

REMEMBERING PARIS

I.

A metro slid in, slipped away, a car
containing people, clean and shiny, dressed
in style to slide and slip in time, on time,
excessive time to primp, compare, regard,
all the time critiquing gleaming, glistening shoes.
Cement filled eyes, then souls accepted the form,
the smoothness, thinking, thinking, thinking, no—
here, no one thought except about their wine
and spendy shoes. The wine and shoes blurred
with metros, smiles eclipsed.

II.

For the last time, the man sat
in the second chair at the corner table
with his hat and coat on,
ready to leave, but remaining

savoring again the Adel Scott he had when de Gaulle left
and several more after his grandson's birth
and the morning coffees on Bastille Days.
He sat and let memories furrow his brow and narrow his
eyes.

He told his wife of the afternoon—
the chairs talking only to themselves,
tables lacking ashtrays and flowers,
inactive air filling the patio.

He didn't mention the mademoiselle in the café across the
street
whose closely shaved legs sucked in stares
as she sat, one leg slightly back,
hair halfway tumbling in her face

the paper in front of her, just another prop
like the Evian bottle—she didn't come to the café for
reading.

ST. ANDRE'S, FRANCE
there were no lights, no men, no language
just wood, God, and me
me, just me
uneasily surrounded by holy water and sacraments

rituals of safety
rituals of comfort
rituals of avoidance
looking at a crucifix
wondering, wondering
praying
perhaps crying
waiting
waiting for the rituals to work for me

The handful of times I voluntarily peeled myself from my mattress on Sunday mornings and went to church, I wanted to find solace and comfort in singing and the drumming. I had great hesitation about attending church. In some instances, the village looked at me as a role model, a mini-American ambassador. They watched and discussed everything I did. They even studied my trash. Some missionaries in the south of Benin had hung posters in villages equating belief in Jesus with monetary gain. I never expressed that sentiment, but I knew that as a wealthy individual in the community, when I worshipped in church, I perpetuated that misconception.

However, I still went sporadically. After the first time or two, my humiliation at dancing up to the altar diminished. Sometimes, in the midst of my solo booty-shaking, I let myself be fooled that the Africans' clapping was because I actually had rhythm and that the drummers actually appreciated drumming for me. I had always wanted to be a dancer on Broadway. A small bamboo structure in West Africa that had no lights or floor worked well as a substitute.

Unfortunately, church became a little too participatory. The villagers started to think I threw myself into the singing and dancing because the spirit of God had found me. Possible. I would not have said "Spirit of God," but my motivation to sing and connect and release and their need to release and believe life would fairly resolve itself probably sprang from the same source.

After the twenty minutes of dancing, I endured the rest of the service because scheme as I might during the week, I could never devise a plan that let me leave inconspicuously. I toyed with the idea of a fake diarrhea attack. However, that would mean church would reconvene at my house after the real service when all the women would stop by to see if I needed anything and to suggest I eat charcoal, or send for my husband. And no matter how hard I tried, or how "late" I arrived at church, people always arrived later or some thoughtful soul would notice me take a place on the bench in back and quickly make room for me up front, waving her hands and calling my name until I moved up closer.

One Sunday, having surrendered myself to the fact that the church contained an unlimited number of kind souls who would help me find a seat no matter when I came, I arrived at the bamboo structure at the official start of the service, which by African time, meant early. An older woman cuddling a creased Gideon's Bible rushed over to me, interlacing her hand with mine, and pulled me into the midst of a group of women fervently repeating a Bible verse. I joined them, repeating the Bible verse until everyone memorized it. I enjoyed seeing how the verse translated. In fourth grade, I had won my youth choir's Alphabet Bible Verse Memory Competition, where participants had to know a verse for every letter of the alphabet. The verse I had just learned in Fon was the very same one that had helped me win in South Dakota: Revelations 7:16.

Fifteen minutes later, as I used my purple sweat rag to dry my face, we took our places on the backless, wooden benches, and the singing started. After the song for the offering, the minister announced that the church had a special treat today. He called my name and asked me to stand and repeat the Bible verse I had learned in Sunday School. Ecstasy radiated from the woman and her Gideon Bible. I didn't move. So, slower, the minister repeated what he said and Mrs. The Woman With The Gideon Bible Who No Longer Had A *Yovo* Friend frantically gestured towards me to stand up. I, pretending my dancing part on Broadway now had a speaking part, dutifully stood and repeated the verse: *Never again will they hunger;/ never again will they thirst./ The sun will not beat upon them,/ nor any scorching heat.*[2]

During the sermon, the minister periodically called on me for confirmation of his points, or to add my own perspective. Problem: I daydreamed during the sermon. The Red Sea, the Ten Commandments, Gabriel, I knew all those stories from childhood. When the heads of the worshippers simultaneously turned towards me, following his voice, thundering in my direction, asking me if what he had said about the Word of Our Lord and Savior held truth, I looked at the expectant faces around me, failed to recall his words, but said *"oui."* People clapped.

REGRET
I closed my eyes and recalled
the burrito next to the Dr. Pepper.
Every wedge of tomato surrounded
by cheese chunks and sour cream pouring
out of the edges of the tortilla onto the wrapper.
With nonchalance, I carried the tray with the wrapper
and its random cheese chunks and sour cream blobs
to the trash container. It opened and I shoved
into its depth the wrapper,

unlicked.

Random questions cross my mind often here. Today: What turns must life take in order for one's occupation to involve getting naked, crawling into a maggot filled latrine and emptying it bucket by bucket?

When I moved into my cement square, it had no latrine. The school promised Peace Corps and me that they would dig me one. They did, a vast abyss of six feet dug into swampy ground. I had had only sporadic breaks from giardiasis and dysentery since my arrival. Almost constant peeing out my ass, combined with the rainy season, overwhelmed my latrine in no time. I had to squat over a coffee can or magazine ad to relieve myself then dump it close to my latrine in the part of my house with no roof.

One morning, I crawled out from under my mosquito net and started the sweat-shuffle down the hallway to the latrine. As I rubbed my ear that had fallen asleep because I slept with the bottom lobe folded up so I wouldn't hear the mosquitoes buzzing, my half-open eyes noticed white on the cement. The usual morning obstacle course consisted of dust balls, dead cockroaches, and mouse poop—all brownish. I used my continuously strengthening thigh muscles to squat and peer at the speck: a maggot. A what? (Another random question…it was early. Perhaps I was having mefloquin induced hallucinations?) I nudged it with my flip-flop. In standard maggot fashion, it hunched up. *Shit.* I scanned my hallway. It had friends. Turning my Nigerian flip-flops into toe-shoes, I daintily maneuvered down the rest of the hallway and looked into the part of the house that had no roof. A thin blanket of white wriggled, hugged the cement, and emitted an odor.

Due to teacher strikes, the director had postponed classes for a while. Still, I draped myself in one of my frumpf-frumpfs and biked off to school with the hopes of finding him, or anyone who could help me rid my home of my new roommates.

At school, I only found the accountant who asked why I had shown up. I explained my latrine had exceeded capacity. He made me repeat what I said saying he could hardly believe my latrine was full since I had only been in my house for just over a year. However, ecstatic at the chance to see *yovo's* house, he agreed to come with me and check out the situation.

We arrived at my house, he first because he took his moto, and I later with my bike in high gear. He sauntered down the hallway, pointing out that it was strangely empty of maggots. However, the maggot carpet in back had gone nowhere. The accountant looked at all the maggots, declared my latrine not full. He reminded me of the rainy season. When the dry season came, in several months, they would go away.

I sensed a chance for cross-cultural growth and an opportunity for me to be less American and more understanding and not mind the maggot situation and say, "OK, I'll wait several months and continue shitting in a coffee can and peeing into baggies and on the faces of world leaders in *Newsweek.*" But I couldn't. I said I didn't want to wait several months. I wanted the maggots gone...*now.*

He tried diplomacy, asking me what we would do in America to solve the problem. I tried to explain flush toilets and sewer lines and purification plants. My valiant effort went nowhere. As he revved his moto outside, he promised to talk to the director about the problem.

On Thursday, school still had not started, and the maggots still squirmed out back. I gave up the battle within myself about cultural understanding. I biked to the director's house, interrupted his nap and told him that if the maggots weren't gone, I was. I was twenty-three, college educated, and I did not come to Africa with the intent of supporting some kind of bizarre, stinky ecosystem in part of my house. I came to teach. Africa made me feel like a hybrid cow/dog, something like Ringo our sheep dog.

The next day he arrived with a bottle of stuff from the Nigerians at the market. Supposedly, the toxicity of the potion warranted his wrapping it in several layers of paper and holding it at arm's length. I smiled as he explained the level of lethal ingredients in the liquid, said it frightened him and assured me that by tomorrow, all the maggots would be dead.

I bounded from under my mosquito net the next morning to see the effects of his super-toxic-close-to-nuclear potion. Maggots maggots everywhere. I sighed, then started talking to them. I hinted that Glazoué had other, nicer latrines. They should not feel obligated to stay in mine. I really, truly would not be offended if they moved. They stayed.

During the weeks that followed, I learned that slimy and squirmy latrine maggots could become my friends. The lat mags, despite having a slight odor, were not as repugnant as I had first believed. They slipped and slid around in nutrients most graciously and plentifully provided by me, and, therefore, without reproach or judgment, they listened when I talked, never cutting me off mid-sentence to go take care of some pressing external issue or offering me cow skin to fix my problems.

Charles came to visit. Papa Rachidi liked Charles. Whenever he saw him, he started talking to Charles about his Force and how he could tell that Charles really had the Force that made me happy.

His monologues about men and their Forces lasted hours. Papa Rachidi said that he himself had the Force that could handle many women. He was sure Monsieur understood. He liked to lecture Charles on how a man couldn't let the Force rest or it would lose Power, and then he wouldn't be a man. He always said it was a good thing Monsieur came to visit because even if Monsieur was using the Force in his own village, Madame *Yovo* had been in need of the Force. Yes, the whole village had noticed she had been tired. And last week she had been sick. Diarrhea. And he would inevitably make the link between sickness and lack of sex…that's what happens when a woman doesn't experience the Force often enough. Why he had even suggested to Madame, that she should look for the Force in Glazoué, perhaps even here in her concession. Papa Rachidi was sure that Charles understood that he had just been trying to be helpful, but Madame had gotten angry and walked away. That too happened to women without the Force; they were easily upset.

And then Papa Rachidi would invite Charles and various other village men to drink and continue to talk and toast their Forces. And since I didn't have a Force like theirs, I left and talked to my latrine maggots who didn't pray for me to have kids or toast a Force.

Charles liked toasting his Force, but he did not like the coffee can situation. I didn't think it helped him view me as feminine either, definitely not potential wife material for back in the States with the other wives of his upper-class friends.

I knew the director of the school did not worry himself at night over the state of my latrine; so I took pictures of my latrine and found a bush taxi to take me to the capital to see the officials in the Peace Corps bureau. I needed help with the situation before I forgot I was human, a woman, dignified. My baggie had a hole and leaked, and I no longer felt a rush of pride when I aimed well into the coffee can, which had started to rust.

On the way out of town, hope flourished. Soon I could squat over an empty, clean latrine. Additionally, my bush taxi driver pointed out that there were now two, not one, but two poles for electricity in Glazoué. Of course, the electrical company had not attached lines to those poles, and they had not left piles of other poles, but the situation had more promise than before. The driver thought electricity would reach Glazoué before Christmas. I started thinking about hunting down Christmas tree lights in the capital and then hanging them in my house. What a wonderful life—an empty latrine and electricity.

The marché mama in the taxi chortled and told me the driver lied. Everyone knew the electrical company only put up the poles to keep people from bitching. She said they wouldn't come back 'til next year. And then it would only be with one more pole. I had to hope that the system moved faster with latrines than it did with poles.

I talked with my Peace Corps director, linking my self-image to dogs. She immediately typed a letter for my school saying what I had already said weeks ago–clean the latrine or *yovo* leaves.

The school read my letter. The director sighed and explained again that when the rainy season ended, the maggots would be gone. I swore as I biked home. The maggots continued to prance.

I found another bush taxi to take me to Dassa. I called the capital to tell them of the maggots' victory. Amazingly, Peace Corps pulled out all stops and sent to Glazoué the ultimate weapon: the SUV with the American flag on the side. I loved Peace Corps cars. I had never understood why men in the States loved cars. Loved to look at them. To talk about their shape and their engines and their capacity. Here, I got more excited about seeing a Peace Corps car than I did Charles. It symbolized control of climate, cleanliness, America, the flag and everything that went with it. That big mobile part of Americana roared up to the front of my school, commanding respect.

However, not only the car commanded respect. With the car came Mathieu. Mathieu was the man, the bad ass, Mr. T. from the A-team. I had never seen anyone toy with Mathieu. He came into town, driving a little too fast, revving the engine a little too much, and stepped out of the car a little too deliberately. Attitude. He molded the words *respect* and *abject fear* nicely. Possibly, the SUV sustained three-fourths of Mathieu's attitude, but I never asked, because I, like everyone else, feared Mathieu. Mathieu did not even talk to me. He exchanged words in the local language with my director and then roared off into the African horizon.

The next day, a delegation arrived at my house and decided not only that my latrine had indeed reached capacity, but also that something needed to be done about it. They located a villager, who, for a whopping sixteen dollars, got naked, crawled into my latrine and my shit and hauled its contents out.

No one in my concession talked to this man whom I considered a hero. Normally he only cleaned latrines during the night so no one could see him and then later identify him as a latrine cleaner. He emptied mine during the day because as the director explained to me, a single woman could not have a strange man in her house at night, unless I wanted the director himself to stay with me for a night. I declined and the latrine emptying began.

Was there a sound more beautiful than the slosh of buckets coming out of my latrine?

FOR ANGELA
It's latrine poetry,
It's raunchy.
Why not?
It's Africa.

My farts raunch,
my shit raunches,
why not poetry that raunches
and rollicks through the mosquitoes

that are far from me—
maybe because of the Cutter's
but I think it's a gift to you my friend

that an ocean separates us—
then only one of us realizes:
without you,

life stinks.

The Beninese professors said the government still owed them wages from 1992, and they wouldn't teach until they got paid something. They started a teachers' strike. Because Peace Corps paid me, every morning I tried to inconspicuously bike off to school, sending mental messages to the people I met on the paths to convince them that they didn't really see *yovo* biking off to have class.

Since not all of my students showed up during the strike, my classes were smaller, thus giving me more leeway with my activities since I didn't have to worry so much about controlling chaos. I brought a map to school to teach the names of countries. After taking attendance, I was disappointed to see that the strike had not kept many of the boys from class. Taking the map out of my bag, I turned to tape it to the wall.

The usual chitchat that began when I turned my back started this time with Ikilou and Wilfried taunting Rachidi. However, after three seconds, instead of the expected crescendoing into a ruckus, the boys became abruptly quiet. No one tapped a pencil. No one drummed a machete on the floor. I sensed no movement at all. Out of the corner of my eye, I glanced towards the door expecting to see an official from the Peace Corps, readying myself for a surprise teacher evaluation.

Several months of teaching had pointed out my naiveté in thinking that my students were going to ferociously gobble up my English lessons. The respect and the attention that I was experiencing at the moment usually came as a result of something external and had nothing to do with my efforts in front of the room, something like the arrival in a cloud of dust of the Peace Corps SUV. I couldn't compete with that. Not even my attempt at quelling the obstreperous antics of Wilfried by copying the commando methods of my colleagues had brought quiet or respect to my classroom. He came to the front of the room and obediently kneeled on a pencil, rolling his eyes and pleading in mock pain, "Madame, Madame, please, *ça m'a fait mal.*" Dismissing him to his seat, I blamed the incident on heat stress. I didn't like what I had just done. But the incident had not fazed Ikilou and Rachidi. They continued their verbal bantering; all the while their feet tapped their machetes on the concrete floor.

This time no dust boiled into the classroom momentarily hiding the shiny SUV. Without moving my left hand that was holding the map to the board, I slowly turned my head a bit, suspecting one of the legendary jumping snakes to have materialized in super-sized form. No snake. No SUV. Ah, was it possible that my students were actually intrigued with the upcoming lesson? Had I finally connected? I turned to face the class directly, and my gaze was met head on by statues. The silence stood for several beats. Finally, Ikilou asked, "Madame, what is in your hand?"

"This?" I said as I held up my right hand.

"Yes. What is that?"

I started to explain that it was a $1.89 plastic tape dispenser from the States, but then I remembered sorcery.

Without explaining anything, merely saying it was something I had the power to use, I proceeded to pull and tear, pull and tear. They, without a pull of a braid or a shove off a bench, watched in awe as I pulled and tore four pieces of tape to finish hanging the map. I gently replaced the dispenser in my bag, having gained some respect from my students for my "power." I gained respect for the importance of little things.

Wilfried and Rachidi, of course, wanted the tape dispenser. I told them for two basins of water, I might consider a trade. To me it sounded fair, but the boys walked away dejected. Water had become a luxury since the rainy season would not start until April, and some wells were already dry, which helped to explain the life expectancy here—Darwin's survival of the fittest.

I survived, but not because I was fit. By village standards I was rich and could afford to pay Akala and Pelagie to walk great distances after class to find water for me. Even though I shared with them, the imbalance of power and privilege remained starkly clear. It bothered me. When Mama Inez had malaria, and I didn't give her my Fansidar, I had the same queasy feeling. I wished my selfishness showed itself in less blatant ways.

Two days earlier, I had missed another opportunity to be generous. I had received a care package with a small container of Velveeta cheese. I never ate Velveeta in the States, but now, it equaled Camembert. I drooled at the thought of a cheese sandwich.

Unfortunately, the village had no bread; so I waited. The next day, still no bread. My willpower vanished, and I decided to eat cheese as cheese, just a couple of small bites as a bedtime snack. The morning might bring bread. Into my third bite, my stomach signaled that, having had no dairy products in months, I had made a bad decision. Partly because I was too tired and partly because it comforted me, I rewrapped the cheese and kept it in bed beside me. After all it had come from America, from someone who cared about me.

At 3:01 a.m., something brushed my arm. Something rustled. I grabbed my glasses and lit a match. A rat. His pokey nose was inside my cheese wrapper! It didn't bother me so much that the rat was in bed with me, but it enraged me to think that he was munching my cheese when I had no possibility of replacing it. I grabbed the rat and threw its furry body into the humid air, cursing myself for having slept with the mosquito net up. While it snaked away, I gingerly picked up the remaining soft lump of cheese, recited a eulogy and heaved it over my wall into the swamp.

As I left the next morning to once again become a scab, Big Mama asked why I had been stomping around in my Tevas during the night. I explained the rat/cheese fiasco. She too was upset. She scolded me. I had let a rat get away.

Tuesday	Wednesday (marché)	Cotonou on Friday?
wrte hme, Angela	tapioca	call hme,
plan class	tomatoes, garlic	stop at med-unit for
visit Big Mama	bananas?	antibiotic ointmnt
if water, wsh sheets if	henna	buy oil, TP, popcrn
not, sweep sheets	candles	

Outside the post office, eleven dead birds walked by in a basket on Ikilou's head. The stench escaped everyone but me. He bargained: three birds for my sunglasses. I said I needed at least six. In the still air, poverty swarmed. Ikilou continued negotiations and walked me to the marché. There, red gods danced in a whirl and twirl of dust, trash, and sweat-shiny skin. When no one threw coins, the god keepers swung bamboo rods. People screamed. I bolted with the crowd. My mind forgot letters that hadn't arrived. Ikilou's birds got trampled.

Dear Angela,
    The BBC does not grace my list of friends.
In addition to their special hour-long program
on the pizza industry, complete with cheese
details, last week they had a special about
chocolate.

In twenty-three seconds, a wet plastic basin dried in the sun. A boy by the onion stand sang *"teinte, teinte,"* flapped his arms to work magic—entice me to throw money near the callused feet that brought him to the *marché* every Wednesday while he carried a basket of rice on his head.

"It's white, like you," he said. I did not give a franc or even laughter in response. He scuttled into the crowd like the swamp lizard in my latrine. I pedaled home, the sweat and dust not darkening my glow. Children scrambled to the path chanting *"white girl, white girl."* I shut my door to stand encased in my concrete house, with its blue paint, imagining being engulfed by the Mediterranean Sea.

The school director had given me a tour before I moved in. "Because you live alone, we built a high, solid wall in back by the swamp. No one will trouble you," he said and left assured I would sleep at ease behind my dirt stained concrete wall which couldn't, though tall, keep out the tops of palm trees, the clouds, the stars, the chanting, or the whacks of bamboo rods on flesh.

For two years, Abilé boasted
he would take three wives
and father 18 children, but only seduced
his domestique—barren.
Abilé's neighbors told him
no woman ever came to a man
who did not sacrifice
fat chickens or a goat.
Abilé listened,
then stole two fowl—
silenced their squawking
with his machete on an altar
and raised his arms crying,
"Gods—End my trial!!"
The gods listened,

sending him a mosquito
infected with malaria
which bit,
answering Abilé's
and the village women's prayers.

FOR LOVE OF THE MOON
I have sat and wondered
and contemplated, scratched mosquito bites,
taken shits in my latrine, glimpsed bats swoosh
between stars and still reached no conclusions
about why or what next.

I wrote about my environment,
describing it in rhythmical, witty remarks
that brought laughter and comments
about "that girl." But in the dark
on my straw mat listening to frogs
that sounded like metal cutters, only I sat.

Afi said her father
might not let her continue school.
The cage of heat I slept in barred rest
again, the third night.
Noises other than bat wings
and lizard tails scraped my door
after the sun went away.

If you knew those things,
would you write?
I had lofty ideals for helping humanity,
making myself a better person.

You didn't give a damn.

In this abrasive air, darkness of dust particles
that chafe my cheeks, I continued

for love of the moon.

COMPLICATIONS
happiness
contentment
rejuvenation

Let them be because of the full moon,
my clean skin,
a comforting letter

and not because of Afi's smile,
or laughter,

or her falling into my hug.

Dear Angela,
    I want to go back so much I'm afraid I'll
never go forward.

Monique Maria Schmidt

RAINY SEASON
starlight swam through my fingers,
ignited the cigarette, reflected my sin
back to heaven, gourds of palm wine
had rivered down my throat—phosphorescent
veins

under the moon my silhouette stroked
the splintered latrine door

it reeked of shit

torso wrapped in cloth, bare shoulders supporting
freckles, I confronted my shadow

remembering soft hair, smooth legs

traced my curves on the slats

bare toes danced on the mud
path, a head rush swirled the stars,
I tripped, scraped my pinky, blood
freed

I entered, squatted

searched the woodgrains
for the flash of my smile

somewhere a chastised puppy yelped

I fanned moonbeams into my sweat

planks
of the door
sliced
palm trees and stars above
a domestique as she swept

my stomach cramped, foreshadowing
more latrine trips

morning and night the palm leaf broom
swooshed sand

it congregated, wind and rain
ensured dunes created became displaced

in each nourishing downpour
the palm leaves frayed, ripped, and rotted

on the deserted trail, I cornered the memories
of cookies—their crumbs floating
in cold milk—and your kiss

spiders stumbled up
my leg hair, angels hung backwards
off clouds, the images evaporated

more quickly than sweat

7

Seven Moon Beams

Y2K

I could now cross Africa off my list of goals. However, I still had not ever received a New Year's Eve kiss. I had thought this New Year's with Charles. But he had dumped me, elegantly saying he wanted to put no more effort into a relationship, the last night of our Christmas vacation.

Usually, because of bush taxis, I arrived in a highly charged emotional state at Beaker's. This time, I arrived crying, trying to pretend to be happy to be with her, not Charles, on New Year's. Eventually, I didn't have to try. I was happy to be with her, and I was happy to be barefoot, wearing nothing but a green and white *pagne* wrapped around me from chest to mid-calf, listening to her walkman on high volume through seven dollar Walmart speakers someone had sent in a care package and dancing dancing dancing in the dirt with Afi and her laughter. Drinks, dust, darkness.

My soul needed to smile. I needed to find my love. So I sang. I stomped my bare feet into the African soil. I threw my arms up like the village women and I sang. Beaker sang. Afi learned. We circled. We stomped. We shook, created a ruckus, woke up the roosters, woke up the universe. For suspended minutes, we were not African or American. We were not young, scared, or scarred. We were sacred. Souls. A soul.

And what I wanted to get rid of from Kyle and from Charles and from Africa and from home, I threw through the jostling night particles to the stars. And my arms grabbed pieces of the silvery white heart tissue of night, speared on the same particles, and brought them back and pushed them into my chest, refilling my heart. My throat opened to the wind and my heart thudded in tandem with the rhythm of life in Beaker's pounding legs and Afi's song. Laughter, latrines, life 2000.

New Year's Eve day we biked to Afi's birth village to visit her family. She was excited. I was hung over. Beaker had bought material and had matching dresses made for herself and Afi. All day we ate. Goat head, *ignam pilee,* rice with sauce, oranges, peanuts. Surrounded by thatched roofs, we greeted her father, her mother, her uncles, aunts, cousins, nieces, nephews, more cousins and aunts and uncles, her father's other wives, her father's other children. Beaker took pictures of everyone. Smiling, arms around her shoulders, Afi thanked Beaker for helping her go to school. Her father shook Beaker's hand solemnly and thanked her also. All the aunts, uncles, cousins, and wives standing around clapped. Someone went into the dimness of a thatched mud hut and found more peanuts to pass around. Another someone found warm sodas to give us. I took a picture of Beaker and members of Afi's family.

Afi stayed in her village. Her father's first wife wanted her to help with the kids until classes resumed. Beaker and I biked back, stopping frequently because of sideaches. Well-fed, happy, we didn't talk during our rests. I dug out my sweat rag and attempted to dam the continuous streams of perspiration flowing from the crinkles on my forehead. We only had seven or eight months left in-country. Afi anchored Beaker, but how strongly? Next New Year's Eve where would we celebrate? Where would Afi celebrate? Would the next volunteer, if there was one, take care of her? Small questions. Details. Realities. Too much.

Though I had never seen it play, Glazoué had a soccer team. The students always talked about their team. To me, they pointed out that they played barefoot, asking if I could get Nike to ship over some shoes. I agreed to write a letter to Nike, but never did. Evidently the team practiced at the school on weekends. I never went to the school grounds on weekends to see them, but I remained perplexed as to how they got their fathers to let them leave the manioc fields for the soccer fields.

When the high school in Abomey, an hour and half away, announced its regional soccer tournament, soccer fever hit my school. With a bush taxi, it cost 1200 CFA per person to get to Abomey. My students didn't even have the twenty-five CFA for school lunch. However, the students had to flaunt their sportive abilities in Abomey. Someone's cousin in Dassa, a neighboring village, had said that Glazoué only had poor people and, therefore, would never progress. Not going to the tournament made that statement appear true.

Dassa did not have much to boast about when compared to Western cities, or even Benin's capital, but when compared to Glazoué, it did. It had electricity, phones, running water, and flush toilets, and a bigger high school. For the honor of their small dusty moonlit paths, and their numerous latrines, and steady candle sales, the students of Glazoué brainstormed ways to get to the tournament. Eventually, someone found a friend who had a friend who knew someone who knew a taxi driver who agreed to take them all, eighteen, in one station wagon.

Abomey, the historic city of kings of Benin, had a red brick wall because they supposedly used human blood to color it. Another wall, which details the history of the kings, depicted one of their favorite methods of torture: bending a prisoner over and shoving dirt up his rear-end until he died. The historic area of the town also contained a grave where ancient people buried four women alive in order to show respect for the king. In orientation I was told that in one of the tombs of a king, four live women, chained, still continuously crouched on all fours around an empty bed. Abomey: the ideal city for a high school soccer tournament.

Saturday morning, at eight, on time, the first layer of students piled in. When situated, the next layer stacked themselves on top of the first. The weighed-down 1974 faded yellow station wagon peeled out of the schoolyard as well as it could with its cargo and worn tires. Jubilation. Singing. Small pats to check to make sure their *gris gris* still hung around their necks. The road to victory, or at least a good time out of Glazoué.

Two weeks before, a neighbor had cursed the driver. He expected the quality of his life to disintegrate rapidly. It hadn't. Eighteen kids had wanted to rent his bush taxi. Even at a reduced price, he was still making money. He began to believe it had been a weak curse, or possibly a joke. However, the popping noise of the right rear tire reversed his earlier decision about the curse. In an instant, he knew the popping sound was an evil spirit announcing its arrival in his station wagon. The last sound before his death. The driver did not want to die.

He didn't try to steer the car, to keep it on the road, or brake to slow it down. He opened his door and jumped out. He rolled along the side of the road as his car careened, no back tire, no driver. Did the kids scream? Did the ones in back see the car cross into the other lane, slamming into the semi in front of them?

After the impact, no one had the option of calling 911, or a hospital, or an ambulance service. Cars came along, stopped. Looked. Women grabbed their *foulards,* shrieked the names of students into the blaze of the morning sun and sank to the shoulders of those around them or surrendered their bodies to the dirt. As the driver picked himself up and walked off into the horizon, someone opened a door of the station wagon.

The kids in the back with other kids piled on top of them survived. Mangled, but alive. I went to Cotonou to see them in the unair-conditioned hospital with its fly covered hallways. One had her jaws wired shut, one lost legs, one an eye, one was comatose–all waiting for some miracle that would produce a surgeon who could help them. I inhaled the humid bloody-fever air, suppressed a vomit reflex, and thought how lucky the dead ones were.

This time I did write a letter, not to Nike, but to my friends and to my father's church. Money arrived. Each time I planned a trip to the hospital, the humid stench of the sick swelled up in my nose and I dry heaved. Instead, I hiked to a house in Glazoué and presented the money to the father of the girl with the jaw wired shut. She seemed to be the one most likely to survive and function in the world again, assuming a surgeon could be found. Her family searched, sacrificed, prayed, sacrificed, asked me to help more.

When the hospital in the capital became too expensive and the family in Glazoué had to borrow money to pay for rice for dinners, they hired a bush taxi with a driver who said he had never had an accident to bring her back to Glazoué. As her mother helped her shuffle up the dirt walkway to the room she would share with her grandmother, below the noise of her heavy nostril breathing, her mother crooned to her: *Someday I tell you, someday I will find a surgeon and you will talk again. Someday, you will sing. I will hear my baby's voice again. Someday.*

The driver had not completely disappeared. When they found him, he said as he jumped from the car he had had a vision: someone had cursed all of Glazoué. I did not know why the people believed him, but they did. Fetishers made money, stockpiling bottles of gin the people brought for payments if they didn't have CFA. People were scared. I appeared to be the only one upset. Disregarding the fact that he killed students, I could not forget the hospital and its odor: slowly curdling blood, stagnant sweat, simmering urine, moist fear. It was not a place of healing. Somewhere vultures lurked. And the patients knew it.

No one prosecuted him. One afternoon, trying to swallow slowly some thick, starchy semi-liquid corn *akpan* on a bench next to Big Mama, I tried to reason with her saying that, realistically, not all of Glazoué could be cursed. She shushed me viciously, a distraught fear gripping her eyes, anger pushing her dark words towards me. She informed me that if the spirits heard me telling her not to believe in them, they would punish her. I shushed.

I slowly biked home from school and gingerly swung my backpack off my shoulders. I had a staph infection in my armpit which impeded movement and made pain a given. A new pastime at night was to use tweezers to pull out strings and strings of puss. So far, the longest unbroken string of puss had reached past my elbow. I boiled water every morning and dipped gauze in it, placing the hot bandage on the sore, hoping to draw the infection out. Charles had had a staph infection once, and the med unit had told him to try the hot water therapy.

As I wheeled my Trek across the concession to my door, Akala's father dragged her inside their house and started slapping her for being late getting water. I felt my sanity start looking for its sandals so it could leave.

Inside my house, I parked my bike under the curtains with the yellow fish and walked over to a locked metal crate which I had bought from the Nigerians at the *marché,* the ones who had given me a lower price after I promised one of them could marry my sister. I unlocked it, dug under my passport, my camera, my film, my college transcripts, and found the key to staying sane: my credit card. I caught a bush taxi down to the capital and checked myself into a hotel with air-conditioning, hot water, toilets, showers, telephones, and cable television. It also had room service and pizza.

Entering the lobby of the hotel, I felt like Julia Roberts in *Pretty Woman,* only stinkier and with much worse hair, puffy snarls after the five-hour ride with no windows. I sashayed. I didn't give a damn how many French government workers stared at me as I dragged my blue plaid rice bag up to the counter and set my moto helmet down loudly on the shiny white formica, next to an arrangement of roses. I needed a vacuum zone. A place where Africa didn't exist.

I arrived on Friday afternoon. During the weekend, I gave my bed ten minute periods of rest when I left it to shower or pee or open the door for pizza. That was it. The rest of the time, I hugged that bed, trying to salvage my nerve endings in an atmosphere of clean and comfort and blankets. With the air-conditioning on high, I piled blankets on me and assumed the fetal position. I pretended I had checked into a ski lodge in Colorado.

From my side, I looked at the phone. The thought of dialing all the access numbers made my hands tired. I didn't call home. What would I say? "Hey, Mom and Dad...how's it going? I just about lost my shit today." What could they do? And I didn't want to hear about gardening or complaints about finding parking at the mall. Sometimes when I talked with people in America, I could feel my soul trying to stuff itself into the coils of the phone cord to escape, leaving me alone, a carcass.

I did call for room service pizza twice a day. The first pizza arrived. The room service man smiled at me in my pajamas at four in the afternoon, asked me if I were tired. The second pizza arrived later that same day. I was still in my pajamas. The next day, I ordered another. The man looked at me in pajamas with my unopened rice bag and asked if I were sick. With the fourth pizza and the now dimmed room lights, he asked if he could contact anyone for me. The Sunday pizza came with more concern. What had happened to me? I assured them I just needed rest and would leave that afternoon. To where? To America? No, back to my village.

I stretched for the remote for the first time. I had wanted to drown my nerve endings in silence. No voodoo chants. No screaming kids. No beatings. No begging. No wind-blown rain on tin. No lizards bumping into plastic water bottles late at night. No trembling aluminum pot boiling tapioca. Nothing. Nothing. Nothing. Nothing. I heard my eardrums relax.

Now CNN. It had soundtracks. Clean, polished people with pressed clothes and make-up and chatter. It zoomed in and out of "moments," had commentary on the moments. Then zoomed elsewhere. To Africa. A special report on AIDS in Africa. I turned the sound off and watched the camera go from reporter to sky to village to skinny person to skinny person with sores to funeral procession to a lone child.

I had talked with people in my village about AIDS. They told me it was not a disease; it was a voodoo curse. Or they told me people got AIDS from eating oranges. Foreigners injected oranges with the AIDS virus and then they ate them and got sick. Or foreigners put the AIDS virus on the lubrication of condoms and then told Africans they had to use condoms to avoid the virus. Or if they had to use condoms and, therefore, couldn't have children, the foreigners were just trying to keep the African population from growing. A few people listened, mostly during condom demonstrations on wooden dildos. Perhaps they changed their behavior. Perhaps not.

People in my village disappeared, suffering from the "skinny disease." Monsieur The Man That Made Me Omelets on the side of the road got sick. Fetishers couldn't help him. Soon after, omelets were no longer an option for me. A professor died from the "skinny disease." He had slept with students. They had slept with other professors. Those professors had slept with other students. Those students had slept with their boyfriends. My school: a funeral waiting to happen. And they had laughed when I talked to them about AIDS. When I showed them condoms, they told me they were "too big" to use condoms. When I said that they were killing students by sleeping with them and, therefore, killing the future of their country, all but two guffawed.

On TV, a white doctor walked through an African hospital, filled with AIDS babies, orphans. A professor, an expert, from a major university in the US came on, mouth moving with wisdom and stats I did not want to receive. The camera went back to the still clean reporter, back to the sky, the lone child, and then it was over. Africa and AIDS, discussed, dissected, done in three minutes.

I wondered if I had ever looked that put together when I walked through the village. I wished I had never turned on the TV. I could have had an hour or two more of peace, but Africa now lived in the room. A huge gaping wound. All I had was a little gauze.

FEBRUARY 9TH, 2000.

Out front, someone is sweeping the earth. People don't do that, do they? I don't remember anymore.

Here, the ground gets swept, and I know how to medicate myself for malaria. My legs are hairy and my neighbors carve canoes out of tree trunks or sell smuggled Nigerian gasoline in glass pop bottles on the side of the road. I've got no black pants, no shiny shirt, no three inch heels.

I have a photo book. I look inside and there I am.

On his way down to the capital to the medical unit for severe heat rash, Phillip's bush taxi stopped in my village. Holding my picture book, he reassured me that I still looked like me, only the me got knocked on my ass by a tidal wave.

It becomes almost a sick joke, volunteers carrying around pictures of themselves in the States to show people, to prove they were something else before; they weren't always dirty, frazzled, and bedraggled.

Out front, someone still sweeps dirt.

And I finally understand why Jesus had disciples to wash his feet. When you're not in the mall in America in your Enzos, your feet get dirty.

Dear Angela,

Once, I asked the stars for Under Roos and a summer swimming pool pass, tilting my head back and throwing hugs up into their beams, my heart sucked in their love, smiling, confident, and safe.

Government-Sponsored-Best-Friend-Jenny arrived. I had not been excited. To begin with: her name. I didn't think it sounded strong. It sounded pretty. Feminine. The kind of girl all the guys liked in high school. And if she were an adult, why didn't she go by Jennifer? I didn't think I would like her. I didn't want a postmate to begin with.

I lived in Glazoué. I taught here. Big Mama knew me. Papa Rachidi tormented me. Mama Inez sold me rice and saved me mangoes. I knew when the Oro came out. I knew where the wells were. This was my town. My friends. My life. I had a system. It had taken a year and half, but the village and I had come to terms with one another. I did not want to share. I knew about *akpan, bombas,* the price of *pagnes,* and who to *saluer.* Explaining all this to a newbie would be tiresome. Especially to someone named Jenny.

Peace Corps told me in November that in January, after I had been alone in Glazoué almost a year, they would place another volunteer in the village. She wouldn't live with me or work at the school, but she would work with non-governmental organizations in the area.

Shortly after, Jenny came for a week's site visit. She didn't want a volunteer in her village either. Africa was going to be her experience. She was going to work with "the people," not with another American.

Glazoué was excited. Two *yovos*. Big Mama told me on Monday that she had seen my sister Jenny. I said she wasn't my sister. On Tuesday, Mama Inez said my beautiful sister Jenny stopped by her rice stand. Wednesday, Papa Rachidi came to talk to me after school and asked why I had not visited sister Jenny. I said I was tired. Her host family lived on the other side of Glazoué. It would be a long bike ride. Soon, night would fall. He got his moto and took me to the house where Jenny was staying during her week.

She looked fresh, clean, stylish. She was wearing Levi jeans, platform sandals, earrings, make-up, and a light blue form fitting T-shirt. By now, my best frumpf-frumpf, oversized to allow airflow, had sweat stains. My Tevas were no longer blue, but rather a muted brown.

I walked into the room. Her host family gathered around and smiled. "Look, Madame Monique, you are no longer alone. You have a friend."

A government sponsored friend who had been in Africa for two months and still looked good. I sighed. "Welcome to Glazoué."

"Thanks. I heard there was another volunteer here."

"Yep."

She told me about the social work she had done in the States and what she hoped to accomplish here. She talked about the Alice Walker book she had been reading, asked if I had read it. I hadn't. She explained Africa to me, according to Alice Walker. I was confused, who had lived here longer? Who knew these people?

I suggested we go to a *buvette* for a drink. She said she didn't drink. She asked me if I went to church in the village. I explained I had gone several times, had been made to dance up to the altar, and had decided not to go again. Plus, I had issues when women who didn't have money to feed their kids spent money on new fabric and dropped coins in the offering plate. She said she thought if she explained she didn't want to dance up to the altar, they would understand. I smiled.

She came back in January, still looking good. Every day I saw her, she looked good, American, young. She wore bracelets, did her hair, got the tailor to make her dresses copied out of her *Glamour* magazines. She was winning the battle against her environment. I was amazed.

She didn't really speak French. The village didn't have vegetables. She had a really strong group of core friends she missed back in the States. Her work in the village remained undefined. My students greeted me, not her, when we went on walks. After two weeks in Glazoué, she went to a *buvette* with me and we had some Grand Flags. Maybe we could get along.

The village loved having two *yovos*. Two Barbies. Invites poured in for dinners, for ceremonies, everyone wanted to meet sister Jenny and watch us interact. Those men to whom I had previously declined invitations, saying as a woman alone, I could not dine with them, tried again to have company.

Ikilou, knowing I found voodoo interesting, assumed Jenny would also. When his friends with voodoo connections told him that the Revenants would appear and dance in the evening, he clapped at my door to ask if he could take me and the newly arrived sister Jenny to the festival.

For Jenny, voodoo did not hold the same allure as it did for me. However, she agreed to go. I had been to Revenant dances before. The first time I went, I took my bike not knowing that there would be hundreds of people gathered at the *marché*.

It was impossible to tell what was underneath the haystack-shaped red and black costumes swaying and sweeping the ground. The Revenants were said to be dead people come back to life who couldn't be touched by the ordinary living. Their "keepers" brandished bamboo rods at the crowd, smacking anyone who tried to touch or didn't throw money.

My first Revenant dance had been my first encounter with voodoo in my village. At that time, voodoo interested me, but I didn't believe it. I didn't believe the gyrating costumes were dead people brought back to life. I had a Western Education. I thought the gyrating costumes were people gyrating, and wearing costumes. When my students saw me at the *marché*, they were surprised. Did I know what this was? In hushed tones, keeping one eye on the twirling figures, listening to the pace of the drums, they explained. When their explanation included throwing money, I scoffed. A scam. The voodoo dancers were a money-making enterprise. When the Revenants rushed my area of the *marché* and people started screaming and my students yelled, "Madame, Madame, you must run. Run, Madame! Run!" They ran. I stayed still. First lesson for my village: Voodoo was not real. They did not need to run from the dancers. I would show no fear.

A Revenant and his keeper reached me. Dust made my eyes water, but I didn't move. I didn't throw money. Whack! His keeper swung his bamboo rod up again for another hit. Hiking my skirt and holding my bike, I raced back to my house. Suddenly, I believed.

This time, with the crowds and the drumming, Jenny, Ikilou, and I arrived at the *marché*. We pushed our way to the front row. Once people saw that Ikilou was clearing a path for two *yovos*, the crowd parted easily. Before leaving her house, I gave instructions: "When everyone around us starts yelling to run, we should run. The Revenants get angry when we don't run, and we don't want to make them angry." I had explained

I had actually been whacked, that my *yovo* status meant nothing. I vaguely hinted that we should run because the Revenants, whatever they were, had power. After almost two years of life here, I knew voodoo consisted of more than charms and chanting. I did not understand it, but I respected it.

"Ohhhhhh, Monique," she said, "you have been in the village too long. Voodoo isn't real."

Maybe it wasn't, but the reverence evident at the *marché* mixed with the fear draping over the area like a low storm cloud were. And the fear was contagious. Shining palms slapped the goat skin drums, cajoling them to speak. After twenty mesmerizingly tense minutes, when the Revenants rushed by us, Jenny bowed her head and threw fifteen francs on the ground.

After the Revenant dance, we walked back to Jenny's house. She had new CDs, fashion magazines, good books, and a whole life history that I had never heard. She needed to be introduced to the post office people, learn where to find eggs, and know which carpenter would rip her off. She liked to laugh and though she insisted on being called Jenny, not Jennifer, I had noticed she had vertebrae. This woman wanted to have an impact on Glazoué.

Jenny: rejuvenation, stronger than the ferocious rain that broke the *chaleur* every year. With her insistence, sometimes naive, that life in Africa could be a balance between passionate work and sporadic fun, she awakened a part of me that had gone into hibernation. I understood her thought process and expectations. Our friendship gave me a safe place in Glazoué to be me.

PRINCE CHARMING
Reaching for the calamine lotion
your picture distracted me.

Not actually your picture—
rather the book that holds your picture
inside it and the you inside me
stopped my hand mid-reach
and my mind went back to scratch
the scab of your memory.

I confused the two—
my mother's own love story
and you—
the one who kissed me
before I fell asleep,
just like my mother did
when I was young
and she was telling fairy tales.

Jenny's presence in the village served as the catalyst that started me thinking about America, the friends I would see in several months, the letters they had sent, the changes that had occurred in me. I hoped I was less angry, more patient, more understanding of Africa, more appreciative of America, more knowledgeable of human nature, a better listener.

I had no doubt that I had mastered the physical hardships of Peace Corps, especially ones related to the toilet, but had I really given as much as I thought I would? Had I really learned as much as I thought I could?

Initially, besides reminding me that I had the dreaded and much talked about "readjustment" coming up, having Jenny in the village abruptly reminded me of physical beauty and how I had "let myself go." I had overheard a new volunteer utter that phrase as she sauntered off the plane and looked at the color-fully clad, sweaty group of old and wise volunteers that had been planning for months to arrive in the capital to help carry the new arrivals' luggage and check for fresh dating opportunities.

The new volunteer had sworn that she would never let herself go as we had. Until that point, I had remained unaware that I had let myself go. It was hard to condition my hair during a bucket shower, dangerous to shave my legs, too hot to exercise all the time, and I was too sweaty to wear make-up. Mostly, village life consumed me to the extent that I quit thinking about my appearance. Her comment didn't bother me. My shadow from the moon acted as my mirror and curves made shadows fun. My environment had liberated me.

Through the Peace Corps Rumor Mill I had heard that even Charles had lost the preppy look. He had grown a beard, not because he wanted one, but out of sheer laziness. The Beninese, curious about the beard, asked him many questions. Like the rest of us, Charles' life in the village allowed him time to create. In a letter, Beaker told me he spun a yarn about sprouting the beard in honor of his ancestors' Nordic/Germanic warrior tradition. I had not been aware of Charles' warrior roots. So, now Charles was a soldier, and Jenny was a cover girl.

However, Jenny created more than a reminder of physical beauty. Her enthusiasm and sincere urge to give to the villagers what she could, re-ignited my belief in lifebeauty, something I had believed was primitive and inherent in all humanity before I realized how much passion it took to sustain it and before I realized not all of my fellow humans could be counted on to nurture and embrace it.

Jenny reminded me we came to Africa to *live* beauty. The night at the *marché* with the Revenants showed us Glazoué had space for both of us. Afterwards, Peace Corps consumed Jenny. Her not-yet-sapped energy propelled her to organize International Women's Day celebrations, AIDS workshops, cooking workshops. I used my experience and language ability to help and strengthen her efforts when I could.

When Jenny and I were not visiting Big Mama or bargaining for cloth in the *marché*, in my journal, I wrote how the school system made me cry and how I wanted to flag down a bush taxi and leave the villagers behind, but I also still wrote about the moon, stars, and wind, marveling at the parallels between them and us. Naively, I had thought living in Africa and working with the villagers would help me understand and utilize the connection between nature and myself.

However, my continual need to present life as funny in my letters home combined with my daily frustrations overwhelmed me, and I gave up. I forgot that the light from the moon was actually reflected light from the sun. I forgot I used to puzzle over how it seemed to be such a different light and a different side to the sun no one would see without the moon's surface of reflection. Jenny's need for my help and knowledge reminded me I was more than village entertainment. She became my moon, reestablishing my drive to create connections and understanding.

Generally, that impulse meant creating insight among many, trying to change "the world" and thinking of a big world, not my immediate one. When comparing those goals to what I actually accomplished—my students raised their hands in class; they could conjugate verbs and sing English songs— I felt beaten.

Jenny made me realize my Tevas were wandering from the path of reality. I had forgotten that beauty was contributing on an individual level, being a moon to the girls in the village, and to Jenny. Beauty was writing thank you letters to all who had written me and been moons to me while I was in Glazoué. Beauty was the support from Jenny that allowed me to feel calm enough to think about breath; beauty was the thought that I could smile, that I could run, that I could run and smile and sweat and walk into my classroom and not be afraid; beauty was knowing fear but not fearing it; beauty was knowing I would, in several months, eat a York Peppermint Patty; beauty was a phone call when the connection worked; beauty was a phone call when a friend was laughing on the other end. Beauty was knowing she had a compassionate man to hug her at night; beauty was knowing that another friend had a six-foot-three German to wash lettuce for her dinner; beauty was knowing that she and her German had a jar of quarters for when they had sex, and it was full; beauty was knowing that time was working working working and I would never understand it. Beauty was knowing that I could embrace every morning and every bowl of tapioca; beauty was Akala singing; beauty was the banana woman giving me the local price; beauty was knowing I learned enough tribal language to survive; beauty was knowing the mountains in America would wait for me. I would get to them. Beauty was planning to buy silver earrings for myself; beauty was living out of two suitcases and having one towel; beauty was the thought of fresh mangoes in the morning; beauty was my mother thinking of me because she was my mother; beauty was knowing my sister missed me; beauty was learning I had fallen in love; beauty was me wrapped in a *pagne*; beauty was goat in *piment* sauce, even though I did not eat *piment*, I knew it made people happy.

> *Angela told me—*
> *step outside, plant your feet*
> *on the earth.*
> *Your soul will recognize its roots.*
>
> *You are a little latrine poetry and soul.*
> *Don't be surprised if you sing*
> *to open the trunks of baobabs.*
>
> *At midnight, listen and hear angels*
> *pass through mango trees and cornfields,*
> *rustling leaves, sweetening fruit.*

They come to care for you.
They are always there,
but you have to listen.

On days that the frustrations of teachers' meetings and the language mishmash of student essays overwhelmed me, all out biking saved my sanity. On a particularly bad day, I returned home to find Jenny waiting for some quality time with me, the seasoned-one. We mixed up oral re-hydration solution and headed out to Nowhere.

Getting to Nowhere involved choosing at random a dirt road rutted by the rainy season. We passed several groups of kids chopping in the fields who stopped their work long enough to sing the usual *yovo* song as we rode past. After thirty minutes of hardcore pedaling, my adrenalin waned. The attitude of my fellow professors and my students' lack of skill faded from recent memory; so we turned back to the village. By this time the kids had left the fields and were straggling back to Glazoué. Seeing us on our bikes, they formed a line across the road, not unusual. Kids liked to play chicken with the *yovo* and her bike, but two...? The possibilities were limitless.

We approached the adorable, impoverished African children. The tall skinny kid in the middle raised his machete above his head, changing the normal *yovo* chant to something that sounded like "Cut the *yovos!*" His compadres, following his lead, raised their machetes, screamed the chant and charged.

At that moment I loved my green, dusty Trek mountain bike. Jenny and I barreled through and beyond the herd of screaming munchkins, and eventually they tired of chasing and yelling. Pausing in the middle of the road, Jenny did a reality check.

"Did we just bike through a bunch of ten year olds with

machetes who were screaming 'Cut the *yovos?*'"

"Ummm...yep, we did"

"Was that normal?"

"Ummm, somewhat."

"And you screamed back at them? Did you think it was a good idea to call a bunch of kids bad names?"

"Well, I didn't have a machete, and I didn't feel like stopping my bike for peace negotiations."

"Oh...you'd better stop doing that when you get back to the States."

"Yeah, well, in the States, I didn't usually get chased by a pack of kids with machetes."

"True. They would have shot you."

I mulled over this concept as we stopped to buy mangoes for dinner. My record mango purchase stood at twelve for 100 francs. I never needed twelve (that many in one day spelled disaster to my digestive tract), but I liked haggling with the ladies at the *marché*. I was becoming more confident with the tribal language, and I was an absolute expert at the grunting and throwing my hands in the air in exasperation. Sometimes, instead of biking, I used *marché* experiences to relieve stress, because that was an appropriate place for yelling and stomping and flinging my arms.

Frequenting the *marché* during my first few weeks, I always paid the inflated *yovo* price. I approached the *marché* mama saying, "Excuse me, Madame, I would like to buy some tomatoes please. How much are they?" She always gave me some outrageous price, which launched me into a high and mighty statement about how I was a Peace Corps volunteer here to help her children learn. Then I asked for a lower price. She responded with a grunt and the original price.

Now, I biked up to the *marché,* and with a hint of grace swept my skirt over the crossbar of the boy's bike. I strode up to my favorite *marché* mama, picked up five tomatoes and gave her my price. She grunted, turned away and countered with a higher figure. Replacing the tomatoes on the banana leaf, I grunted in return and in Fon said, "I'm not paying that absurd *yovo* price!" Cranking up her grunts and gathering grunts from her neighbors, she threw her arms in the air while lamenting her tough life in Benin. I, too, threw my arms in the air, grunted, set my money next to the tomatoes, saying in Fon, "Take it or leave it." She took my money, handed over seven tomatoes, giving me a bonus for dramatics.

It had taken me quite awhile to understand the importance of grunting, yelling and gesturing. Completely not Mennonite. Making a scene was vital, which made the hot season especially rough. I didn't have enough energy to lift a glass of water to my mouth much less go to the *marché* and work myself into a dither over five tomatoes.

I finally realized that the only way I could endure the hot season was to become a sorceress. The longer I stayed, the more I saw the benefits I could have had—in the classroom and out—if only I had been a sorceress. From what I observed, sorcery was a win-win business. Farmers paid a lot of money to ensure rains. If a charm didn't work, it was never the fault of the sorcerer; someone else had simply had stronger magic. However, if the charm produced as intended, it meant repeat business.

Shortly after Jenny, my sister arrived. Tickets to Africa were expensive, and my letters home did not always flatter my current living conditions. On occasion, I purposely made Africa sound uninviting. I could barely take care of myself here. I did not know how I would keep my friends healthy and happy if they visited. My friends decided to stay stateside. My sister, however, saved the money, packed a pan of brownies from my mother, and ventured over the ocean to see me and experience Africa. We spent one day in the village.

After a squished, but uneventful bush taxi ride to Glazoué, Fofo and Akala met us to help carry her bags. They set them inside my "aquarium" room, which they had helped dust and sweep. My sister noticed the lizard that sometimes ran around the room. She didn't like it. Akala could tell she didn't like it; so Akala and Fofo found sticks, screamed, and chased the lizard around the room, trying to smash it. Its tail came off. It scuttled out the door. The tail remained. I laughed. My sister didn't. We looked like twins. I had forgotten we weren't.

At night, I lit a candle for her to read. I lit my own candles. The usual bugs gathered and flitted around. One bug bit my sister inside the upper thigh. It hurt. My sister said it hurt an abnormal amount. She couldn't see it. She took my flashlight and went to the latrine to look at it. She said it was swollen. An abnormal amount. She asked if I knew what kind of bug would bite like that. I said no. She wanted to look in my "Where there is no doctor" book. She thought she might be dying. I said I was sure she wasn't dying—but then again? She wanted to take medicine. She didn't want to take the medicine in brown bottles with handwritten labels I dug out of my dusty Peace Corp medicine kit. She wanted to go home. She did not want to die in the dark in Africa.

She was still alive the next morning. However, we went to the *marché* to look at the food and make arrangements for a taxi to take us down south to a French beach resort for the remainder of the week. I didn't mind. The beach was Africa too.

204

8

Three Moons New

I MADE A CONSCIOUS EFFORT TO EXHALE EACH TIME I looked at the banana-leaf basket that holds Charles' letters. Some days I managed not to re-read them. Just as real farms had dogs, real women had boyfriends. I struggled not to hold that as Truth. But intuitively I accepted it as fact. In high school I watched the popular girls rack up votes for Homecoming Queen, while their boyfriends stood basking in their glory. No winning Quiz Bowl member ever pulled in enough numbers.

I joined the Peace Corps expecting a higher level of living. Peace Corps provided an escape, a utopia. The people I met, the projects I developed, the lessons I presented would consume all my thoughts and energy. But I was wrong. Both the local culture and the volunteers magnified the "couple crave."

As first-time volunteers arriving in Benin, we began to think that we were the Last Westerners Alive, an idea that settled mysteriously over us like fog and from which we never escaped. We had to copulate, instantly, often, in order to maintain the species—or at least to keep ourselves alive—or at least to feel cared for—or at least be in a familiar situation. A coping mechanism. A safe one too, since Peace Corps supplied quantities of free condoms. However, African heat weakened the condoms, and they sometimes burst in mid-act, resulting in medical evacuations for some and new families for others.

And for the villagers? I supposed their concern with copulating came from the very real need to survive. And love? I assumed, yes, also, but I didn't know. Briefly, I studied African religions and human sociology in my mostly white, mid-western undergraduate university. I was neither an ethnographer nor an anthropologist, but I threw myself into this experience as a twenty-two year-old human, hoping to learn something about *humanity*. Yet, I spent the bulk of my time thinking about Charles and cursing Kyle. What was wrong with me?

What was wrong with all of us? When the mostly female group of volunteers and I boarded the plane in D.C., I anticipated two years in an unknown environment where we had challenging discussions, learned about West Africa, supported one another, appreciated our diversity, and strengthened the team effort. On occasion we did. However, if the occasion involved men, we didn't. Among this group of competent women, I was not the only one who sought security in sustaining a relationship. Two volunteers quit talking to me because they had wanted to date Charles.

I walked off that plane in Africa not looking for romance, but hoping to contribute, to wear myself down until I reached a point of wisdom. And the wisdom reached? Through Beaker, Charles, Jenny, Akala, Pelagie, Afi and Big Mama, I discovered that certain personalities drew me magnetically to their sides. I loved them instantly, completely, without reservations. I realized that I wanted to be loved, completely, without reservations. And that surprised me. Then frightened me.

Had I come to Benin just to learn the importance of friends, family, community and love? My fellow philosophers would call that hokey. I felt like a Hallmark card. I never doubted that I was courageous and intelligent and ambitious; yet, I would do almost anything to see my self-worth reflected in the eyes of someone else. Was this the earth-shattering, life-altering knowledge that I was supposed to learn? What about insight into Democracy and Colonization and World Equality? I shouldn't have ended up here because of *love*, because I didn't feel loved at home or couldn't find love or didn't want it and, therefore, was making myself useful, valiant and wise in order to be loved or to be above it.

Muddled. The reasons why I came. Muddled. Someone knew. If I couldn't figure it out through my experiences, I could read–Kundera, Plato, Sartre–writers who had never been to Africa or Achebe, Kingsolver, Naipaul–who had been here. They had insights. What was I missing?

I had transformed my aquarium room into a writing room as well. Visiting volunteers now scribbled quotes—inspirational, questioning—with chalk on my walls. The marks horrified Big Mama. Akala and Pelagie wanted to know what the words meant. I translated. They asked why God wasn't mentioned.

When others arrived and left their voices on my silent walls and when Akala and Pelagie came, wanting to understand the echoes left by the squeak of the chalk, I felt happy. Was this the big, important lesson that I was supposed to learn? The one for which I had uprooted myself? That we needed community? That I needed community? The world would work as long as we loved ourselves and helped each other. No matter the circumstances, if we read the world in a beautiful way, we could find beauty. During small patches of good days, I believed that.

We seemed to have been catalyzed by a grand master plan: Isolate the young Americans. Take away their safety zones. Remove the familiar. Frighten them. Make them vulnerable. Make them question...even their bathroom habits. Let them scramble to the capital. Let them drown in a weekend of Hollywood videos and ricochet back to the village no longer knowing what they value or why. Have them reject fluorescent lights and hamburgers but have no desire for candles and goat head. Immerse them in loneliness. Tempt them with physical contact. Instill fear for the raw, sensitive nature of love. See if they break.

Tell them of their importance in helping the village progress. Do not define progress. Let it keep them awake at night. Let them hear Papa Rachidi yell and Mama Inez cry. Let them convince themselves it is beyond their control. Let them write two sets of letters home, only one to be sent. Let them wonder what they wanted here. Let them wonder how the village can give it to them. Let them think about the village and themselves and bite their lips.

And the village? The village. I didn't know what the village thought. I didn't know anyone well enough to be honestly told. They thought that I was playing a game here. They thought that my government sent me here instead of sending me to jail for some unidentified crime. Some of them didn't think of me at all. And they shouldn't have.

AFTER STEIN
we are human nature, humans in nature,
humanity = human, not humane.
humans can talk, humans in nature can talk, it is natural
for humans in nature to talk, to talk about nobility.
Yes, it is natural for humans to talk about nobility, maybe it
is not humane, but it is human to talk about nobly accepting
challenges,
to accept to overcome hardships.

Yes, in nature, it is humanity that talks, talks about impact,
naturally it thinks, not the nature.
No, the nature does not think, at least it is
natural that humanity does think that nature does not
think,

but the humans, they think, they think of life,
but neither the nature nor the humans think life,
neither thinks life thinks, but it gives.
Yes, it gives, gives reservations, life gives reservations, it is
not nature that reserves the humans, life does,
and it is not nice, it is poverty these humans in nature.

Showing neighborly concern, the *gendarmes* sauntered over to enlighten me about the cause of my dysentery: I had no permanent man in the house; therefore, I was not having enough sex. The older one said it would not bother him to help me stay healthy.

I had no idea dysentery and sex were related. I needed to alert the Peace Corps medical unit. They diagnosed my dysentery as a result of drinking un-boiled well water, or the meat/fly-roost I bought from a street vendor, or holding Francis' hand after he left the latrine, or eating both bags of Twizzlers and the package of Oreos in my care package all in a matter of twenty minutes.

The *gendarmes* belonged to the Fon tribe. Glazoué, started by the French, had no true people of origin, but the majority of its inhabitants belonged to either the Fon or the Idaacha. Fon spoke their own language, Fon, while the Idaacha spoke a language similar to Yoruba. The Fon and the Idaacha did not always like each other.

I had no energy to notice which people lived where and why they snapped at certain others. Keeping my dress out of my bike chain while trying to balance a live chicken dangling from my handlebars absorbed all my attention. With no books about the local culture, no TV specials, or fellow Western-thinker as bases for reality checks, everything and everyone appeared strange.

On most nights, the two *gendarmes* plowed through the

dusk on their motos into our concession. Usually Fofo, being the slowest of the many munchkins and, therefore, the last kid left as the others bolted into obscurity, ended up serving as valet for them, wheeling their motos from the concession gate to their front doors while they changed out of their starched forest green uniforms into loose, flowing African cottons covered with prints of chickens and upside down phones—one had an outfit with the Eiffel tower on it. Once air could waft through the cotton, cooling their rolls of belly flesh, they claimed their territory on their straw mats in front of their doors and nursed Grand Flags while waiting for a timid child to glide through the mosquitoes and quietly place bowls of *akassa* or freshly-pounded *pilee* next to them.

However, this week the routine altered. The ongoing quarrel between the Fon and the Idaacha escalated, meaning it finally became apparent to me.

Debating whether to purchase purple and orange Nigerian flip-flops or to save my 1500 CFA to buy ice cream when I went to Cotonou, I overheard conversations about one tribe planting manioc on the other tribe's land. While I mixed my beans and *gari* in the teachers' room at school, one of the professors mentioned that someone had set up a roadblock on a path and actually beat a villager who tried to go through it. The blame for such actions shifted according to whether they were reported by my students, the Nigerians, the women at the *marché*, or the other teachers at school, .

Beatings, roadblocks, stolen land—the *gendarmes* launched themselves into action, starting "strategy" meetings in our concession. Now, instead of the two of them, by eight p.m. a small crowd of *gendarmes* shifted their weight back and forth, crackling their straw mats in the area outside my door. Instead of hearing Fofo and Akala dashing after their rusty tire rim, my night's melody became the rise and fall of men's voices: heavy whispers building to rage, then a sharp shushing, followed by the clink of beer bottles set back on concrete. They strategized

212

for two weeks, but nothing ever happened, other than the *buvette* closest to my house enjoyed increased sales and taxi drivers without papers had several weeks of respite from paying bribes.

When the first strategic council meeting convened, one *gendarme* came to my door specifically to tell me they were having strategy meetings against the Idaacha, and I was not to listen. I reminded him he conducted his top-secret meetings in Fon, and in Fon, I could ask for rice or beans, and inquire about the state of health of his/her family. Unless their counter attack plans included massive quantities of rice and beans, I could not transmit their ploys to the Idaacha. He laughed, repeating what I had said to his "council."

His comrades immediately repositioned themselves on their mats, making room for one more, and invited me to have a beer with them. I declined, explaining that I had a meeting for which I had to prepare. The U.S. Navy was coming to town.

I had submitted a small proposal to the Embassy for Peace Corps funding to improve the school: repair window slats, install doors, mount new blackboards. Glazoué had been denied. My school was crushed. Their pervasive dejection sent me back to ask again if there was any money anywhere leftover from any other projects. I expected a "no," but hearing the "no" in an air-conditioned office would cushion my disappointment.

However, I heard no "no." Instead, the woman in charge explained about the Navy and its Humanitarian Aid, a budget nearly seven times larger than the amount for which my school had asked. I forgot to blink. With that amount of money, we could have benches and doors and blackboards and more. After looking at my proposal, she said to expect a visit in Glazoué so the officers could verify it needed aid.

During my bush taxi expedition back to Glazoué, I devised a plan to work with my students on both etiquette and English. How to speak English *politely*. When the Navy arrived, I did not want the students to chant *yovo yovo bon soir,* or try to show off their talents at making improper metaphors about people being fat as elephants or as shiny as a wet banana leaf. We would show we needed help, and we had manners.

They came. They saw. They took me to lunch at a local *buvette* and let me ride in their SUV. The students stared. But were silent. When the officers crisply stepped into the concrete classrooms, the students slapped their desks, stood, and said stiffly, "Good morning, Sirs." Thirty or forty of them respectfully swarmed around the officers after class to say, one at a time, what a wonderful country America was.

The officers categorized Glazoué as needing aid and gave us enough money to build several new buildings and a school laboratory. Finally. I imagined I heard the village sigh. Finally, having this white woman who biked around and complained about her latrine was paying off. The Navy's generosity overwhelmed me. I wanted to hug the officers, but they were officers, freshly showered and skilled at small talk.

9

Last Moon Dancing

ITʼS REALLY TOO BAD

Madame, your start is something that bothers me! No leave Ikilou! Good Route to USA and good start to your lineage!

Ikilou tore the cover of his math book off and wrote on the inside. I cried. After two years of my English class, he didn't understand what *start* meant. And we had done numerous flash-card drills using the word "start."

At home during my siesta, I heard the roar of the *gendarmes* arriving for food. I stretched my legs, wiped off the dust that clung to the sweat on my elbows, and dragged myself off the straw mat to pull the faded blue and yellow fish curtain back a bit. Leaning my head under a spider web and watching Fofo wheel the *gendarmes'* motos to their doors, tears united with the sweat on my cheeks. This I had not expected.

Akala came to get my plastic basin for water and I cried. I went to the *marché* and bargained for tomatoes with a woman from whom I had never bought tomatoes. I knew that if I bought tomatoes from the regular tomato woman I would cry.

I walked to the center of the *marché* and found a taxi driver who agreed to take me and my luggage to Cotonou the next day. I asked him to pick me up at five a.m., when most people in the village would be sleeping. It would be dark. I told no one what time I would be leaving. No one would see my tears.

The taxi driver talked. Big Mama showed up at my house at seven p.m. "After two years, you just leave. You just leave us here. After two years." To take home, she gave me cassava, and the guilt of her hands wringing a sweat rag wet from tears. That I was not expecting. Big Mama actually really liked me. I cried.

Akala, Pelagie, Fofo, Rachidi, Ikilou, the director, the minister, the *gendarmes* clapped at the doorway. I gave them the traditional water in a bowl, with tears. I couldn't talk. And why? I wanted to leave. I had been waiting to leave for two years. But though I was hesitant to admit it, part of me was imbedded in my blue concrete walls, and part of me waited for the rooster's crow at four a.m. so I could cuss and roll over to sleep for two more hours. Part of me loved Big Mama and smashing palm-sized spiders with my books.

I knew Afi's father slapped her around, and Little Rita's brother forbade her to go to school. The school director had two wives and beat them both. The twelve-year old girl, third row on the right, slept with *Monsieur le Professeur du Historie/Geo.* Mama Inez had malaria, and the villagers burned thieves alive.

But I was going home, going home, home. Buying a ticket, catching a plane, leaving malaria and Afi's father behind.

It was material for storytelling. It was a script for a Sunday night movie. But I was going home, going home, going, gone.

Today, I buy cream cheese at the bagel shop as if that world where goats count as paying passengers and machetes are school supplies doesn't exist, as if a new volunteer hadn't called at 5:25 a.m., collect, from a dusty green pay phone to say Afi had appeared in the capital, as if she hadn't been bleeding, hemorrhaging for three days, raped.

> *"shut de door keep out de devil*
> *shut de door keep de devil*
> *in de night"*[3]

> *I moved*
> *to a different continent*
> *I left*
> *without speaking*
> *but I still wanted*
> *to sing*

As if it hadn't been her first time and the concept of rape existed so justice would be done. As if her uncle hadn't let it happen. As if her uncle hadn't accepted money and then left the house so it could happen.

> *so I taught others*
> *the song*
> *Afi learned*
> *the song, she loved*
> *to sing, she learned*
> *and she danced with me*

As if, while the clerk tells me they are out of light strawberry, there isn't a girl in a mud hut rocking herself, face becoming hardened like the faces of other African women—as if the force of wind and vibrancy of sun have never dashed across them.

as I sang
"shut de door
keep out de devil
shut de door keep de devil
in de night
shut de door keep
out de devil
light a candle everytins alright
light a candle everytins alright"[3]

As if my wanting to be her mother, as if my showing her how people could be loved, trusted, as if my telling her about my world had not just made her easier to rape, as if the man she was told she should trust, the man we said would feed her and arrange her schooling with the money that was left had not just shoved her down in a dark hut and then ground himself into her over and over.

Afi listened to all that
I said to every word
she listened when R.
came in her as the weasel
had cum in me, with force,

As if I hadn't said to her what my friends wrote me when I complained in letters: "have faith, smile, be strong." As if I hadn't left out the phrase, "it's only temporary." As if I hadn't pacified my guilt at leaving, at continually cursing her culture, by pointing to the sky and explaining, "we will still be connected—look at the stars and think of me."

behind closed doors
she cried and she ran
for me, but I
was gone

As if she will forget how we said, "Afi, we must go back to our families but you stay here in your hut that leaks in rainy season, and be starved by your father, and raped by the man you were told to trust. It will be difficult. We will miss you too, Afi, but you study hard, and every night, let the stars remind you of us."

> *"light a candle*
> *everytins alright*
> *light a candle everytins alright"*[3]

I buy light walnut instead and walk out the door.

OCTOBER, AMERICA
There is concrete and carpet.

I need dirt, sun, and wind
ground into me.

I miss the spirits. God,
I miss the spirits—Big Mama's
Afi's, Africa's, mine, the spirit of Life.

God was there, in my face,
day and night, as I laughed,
cried, and then accepted.

Acknowledgements

Every blade of grass has an angel that
bends over it and whispers, 'grow, grow.'
—The Talmud

And then this happened. The book was finished. But whole chapters were missing. Sharp wisdom and steady insight were not included because at twenty-two, they weren't mine.

I have never "gotten over" my Peace Corps experience. Some days it nourishes my soul; some days I worry it will break me. But I have learned not to belittle or fear love and I learned in some instances, love prevails. Due to Beaker's fundraising, Afi was sent to a new school in the capital where she has done remarkably well.

So, this is what happened. (Granted, you already know what happened, but this is the most important happening.) Years later, it was found. The smile was found. I forgave myself. I forgave others. My stories surrounded me, but I let my friends hug me and buy me chocolate. They showed me home. Repeatedly. I cried. I breathed through the fear. I saluted the sun and heard angels again. Then laughter moved in. The smile won. Becoming literate. Everything is round.

Since returning to the States, I have learned much more about Africa and life. However, I have tried to reconstruct my experiences as closely as possible to those of the wondering twenty-two year-old I was then.

I could not have finished writing without the support and encouragement of many wonderful people who deserve recognition for being incredible humans.

Thank you!

My wise writing women: Margaret Himley, for compassion and courage; Nicole Moss, for strength and vision; Linda Hasselstrom and Windbreak House, for providing the rejuvenation I needed.

My East Coast angels: Kokkie, for finding my laughter; Bryan Pruitt, for sharing his city; Barb and Gary Gaspar, Lyn and Drew Nahigyan, and Marie and Jim Vinup for "adopting" me numerous times.

For friendship, wisdom, and motivation: Karla Schumacher, Paul Butler, Anne Fitzsimmons, Dov Stucker, Joanne Pinaire.

My Peace Corps Posse: Boulonh Soukamneuth, Carol Brillhart, Amy Octaviano, Chad Mosier, Kristine Vinup.

The dance crew: Sarah Treado, Wendy Underwood, Erika Iverson.

For good meals: Melissa and Ilan.

For *lamb at the altar* by Deborah Hay: Rahul Mehta and Robert Bingham.

Augie Doggies: Admissions, Don Grinager, Scott Fish, Tim Johnson, Sandra Looney, Mark Van Weinen, Julia Pachoud, Heather Schoolfield, Mike Smith (for the beads).

Steve Wood: for charcoal.

Mary Dejong: for yoga and conversations.

My mom and dad and all their friends and relatives who listened to them recount my stories and then wrote me letters.

My sister, her husband, their basement, Tabby and Macho.

Claire and Joe Sturr, my Syracuse grandparents.

Syracuse MFA, for giving me a writing community and time to read, reflect, and write.

Matthew Himley, for inspiration, encouragement, and changing my world view.

Geraldine Kennedy, for appreciating the stories and taking a risk.

Notes

1. page 55

   Ta parole est une lampe
   à mes pied et une
   lumiere sur mon sentier.
   Ta parole est une lampe
   à mes pieds et une
   lumière sur mon sentier.
   Ta parole est une lampe
   à mes pieds et une
   lumière sur mon sentier.

2. page 164

   Ils n'auront plus faim et ils n'auront plus soif, et le soleil
   ne les frappera plus, ni aucune chaleur.

3. pages 135, 138, 219, 220, 221

   The author presents the lyrics to SHUT DE DÕ as she
   recalled them from her childhood. The correct lyrics follow,
   used by permission:

   Shut de dó, keep out de devil.
   Shut de dó, keep de devil in the night.
   Shut de dó, keep out de devil.
   Light de candle, eve'rythin's alright.

Glossary

agouti	rats
akassa	an entree of chilled white starch, often served in a gumbo sauce
akpan	starchy liquid drink made from corn
allez	go!
au village	in the village
beignets	fried food, generally beans or manioc
bien integre	well integrated
BEPC	school exam
bomba	traditional Beninese outfit, *pagna* on bottom and big shirt with a *foulard*
bon choses	good things
bon soir	good evening
buvette	bar
ça m'a fait mal	it hurts me
C'est quoi?	What is it?
CFA	monetary unit, Central Franc of Africa, no longer in use
chaleur	the hot season
choses-la	thing
concession	communal living area—it used to be one man and his wives, now different families may group together in one area
Cotonou	the economic capital of Benin—the governmental capital is Porto Novo
Devi	the name for a voodoo god who could change into a lizard and burn people alive

225

Dieu Seul Sait	only God knows
domestique	maid
faire du sport	exercise
fansidar	medication to take in case of malaria
Fon	West African tribe and its language
foulard	head scarf
gari	ground, fermented, roasted cassava used to complement food
gendarme	policeman
giardiasis	a water-borne diarrheal illness caused by Giardia intestinalis (also known as Giardia lamblia), a one-celled, microscopic parasite that lives in the intestine and is passed in the stool of an infected person or animal.
Glazoué	name of the village where Monique lived
Grand Flag	brand of beer
gris gris	voodoo (can be used either for good luck or as a curse)
impolie	impolite person
ignam pilee	pounded ignam, a potato-like vegetable
légère	light, buoyant, fleet
les femmes au village	women of the village
marché	market
mefloquin	medicine used to prevent malaria
merde	shit
Mon Dieu	My God
Monsieur le Censure	man in charge of schedule
Monsieur le Surveillant	man in charge of disciplining students
moto	small motorcycle, moped
Oro	voodoo sect

GLOSSARY

oui	yes
pagne	rectangular piece of cloth worn wrapped around shoulders or waist
pastis	alchohol that tastes like black licorice
PCV	Peace Corps Volunteer
pfeffernüsse	Low German miniature hard "cookie" made by rolling dough into ropes and cutting into 1/2 inch pieces
piment	spicy sauce
quatriéme	students in the fourth level of school
quelque choses	something
saluer	to greet
sodabei	very strong homemade liquor
tapioca	starchy, granular extraction from the cassava root, considered a staple, not a dessert
tchouk	strong cheap millet beer
teinte	familiar way to address a young woman
vendeuse	a woman who sells things
viens ici	come here
yovo	foreigner
zemijahn	taxi-moto
zwiebach	Low German bun made by putting a smaller ball of dough on top of a larger one

About the Author

MONIQUE MARIA SCHMIDT was born in Kansas and moved with her family to a sheep farm in a Mennonite community in South Dakota. After completing her undergraduate degree, she studied and worked in France before joining the Peace Corps where she served as an English teacher in the West African country of Benin. She has also lived and worked in Japan, the West Indies and Latin America. With an MFA in creative writing from Syracuse University, she currently teaches composition and creative writing in a university in Colorado and is at work on her second book.

Monique Maria Schmidt debuts her formidable virtuosity as a story teller of moving depth and humor in *Last Moon Dancing: A Memoir of Love and Real Life in Africa*.